S\ ... AND

KET GUIDE

return

ope ... iny this h

it b

Walking Eye
mobile app

Discover the world's best destinations with the Insight Guides Walking Eye app, available to download for free in the App Store and Google Play.

The container app provides easy access to fantastic free content on events and activities taking place in your current location or chosen destination, with the possibility of booking, as well as the regularly-updated Insight Guides travel blog: Inspire Me. In addition, you can purchase curated, premium destination guides through the app, which feature local highlights, hotel, bar, restaurant and shopping listings, an A to Z of practical information and more. Or purchase and download Insight Guides eBooks straight to your device.

TOP 10 ATTRACTIONS

THE MATTERHORN
A challenge to mountaineers from around the world. See page 101.

ENGADINE
Zernez is the main gateway to the Swiss National Park. See page 82.

THE BASEL CARNIVAL
This popular three-day cultural event takes place during Lent. See page 40.

LUCERNE AND ITS LAKE
At the heart of William Tell country. See page 66.

CHÂTEAU DE CHILLON
Austerely beautiful, the old stronghold of Château de Chillon looks out over Lake Geneva. See page 120.

THE JET D'EAU
The tallest monument in Geneva reaches the height of a 40-storey building. See page 105.

BERN
The capital is listed by Unesco as one of the world's cultural treasures. See page 48.

THE BERNESE OBERLAND
This spectacular region of mountains, lakes and glaciers works a special magic on visitors. See page 58.

ZILLIS
Where the oldest painted ceiling in Europe can be seen. See page 81.

TICINO
Its valleys and lakes have an Italian feel. See page 86.

A PERFECT DAY

9.00am

Breakfast
Follow in the footsteps of Lenin, Trotsky, James Joyce and Herman Hesse by having breakfast in Zürich's *Jugendstil* Café Odeon at Limmatquai 2, which opened in 1911. Einstein gave lectures there.

11.00am

Coffee break
Head across the River Limmat to browse Zürich's most opulent shopping street, Bahnhofstrasse. Head to Sprüngli at No. 21 for tasty cakes and coffee.

Noon

Lunchtime cruise
Trams 2, 8, 9 or 11 from the adjacent Parade-platz stop will take you to Bürkliplatz, where ZurichCARD holders are entitled to a 90-minute round trip on the lake from the pier at Bürk liplatz. Disembark at any pier and take a later boat back.

10.00am

Retail therapy
You are well placed to explore the warren of pedestrianised streets north of Rämistrasse where most of the city's interesting shops and galleries can be found. Pick up paintings and prints, antiques, books, toys, musical instruments, collector's comics, and fashion items.

2.30pm

Culture fix
Take tram 11 to Bahn-hofquai for a visit to the Swiss National Museum at Museumstrasse 2 which offers an insight into Switzerland and the Swiss people from pre-history to banking.

6.00pm

An aperitif
Take tram 13 back to Stockerstrasse and hop on tram 8 to Römerhof for the cog-wheel Dolderbahn and the terrace of the Dolder Grand Hotel. From there you can watch the sun set over the lake and the Alps.

10.00pm

On the town
Take tram 3 one stop to Kunsthaus and tram 8 to Stockerstrasse, which will take you to the stylish club Jade at Brandschenkestrasse 25.

4.30pm

Indulge
Take tram 13 to Wafenplatzstrasse for the short walk to Brandschenkestrasse 150 for one of the latest additions to the Zürich scene, the Thermalbad & Spa, in a brilliantly converted brewery. Besides a series of cavernous pools, hot rooms and showers and a great hydro-massage, it offers fantastic views of the city from the rooftop infinity pool.

7.30pm

Dinner
Return on the Dolderbahn and take tram 3 to Neumarkt for an alfresco dinner (if the weather permits) at Restaurant Neumarkt at No. 5. In its quiet tree-shaded garden, you can enjoy imaginatively reworked Swiss dishes.

CONTENTS

INTRODUCTION

A country of contrasts and of great natural and cultural resources, Switzerland is going through a period of important changes. At the start of the 21st century, past and future coexist, confronting and complementing each other in a present that many Swiss see as less perfect than that of a few years ago, with the hint of further socio-political changes to come.

No map can recreate the geographic reality of Switzerland. Nearly two-thirds of the country is mountainous. Some summits are more than 4,500m (14,750ft) high; no one can resist the myths surrounding the Matterhorn (Mont Cervin) or the imposing trio formed by the Eiger, the Mönch and the Jungfrau. To the east, beneath the slopes of the Grisons, lie the prestigious ski slopes of Arosa, Davos and St Moritz. Fertile lowlands, situated between the Alps to the southeast and the rocky green range of the Jura to the northeast, spread in a circle between Lake Geneva and Lake Constance. At once pastoral and industrialised, this narrow band contains all the big cities and the majority of the 7.9 million inhabitants that make up the Confederation.

The diversity of Switzerland, however, goes beyond its landscape and climate, which is Alpine in the mountainous regions and nearly Mediterranean in southernmost Ticino. Cultural currents converge at this linguistic crossroads wedged between powerful neighbours. Three major languages have official status: in fact, some 65 percent of the population speaks *Schwyzerdütsch*, an Alemannic German dialect, while 19 percent claims French as their major language, and 10 percent Italian. A fourth national language, Romansh (1 percent), spoken in some Grisons mountain valleys, owes its

What's in a name?

Suisse, Schweiz, Svizzera, Svizra... the country has so many official names that its stamps and coins cannot contain them all. So they carry its Latin name instead: Helvetia.

The Parliament Building in Bern

survival to the fierce determination of its speakers. Each group has its own traditions, literature, gastronomy and way of life, but there are cultural interchanges – some of them institutional, others more hidden, none of them easy – that make Switzerland a vibrant patchwork of individuals and ideas.

GRASS-ROOTS GOVERNMENT

Politically, a grass-roots democratic system takes account of regional aspirations. Each of the 26 cantons and demi-cantons that make up Switzerland enjoys considerable autonomy, as do some 3,000 communes, both rural and urban. Popular initiatives and referenda are used on the local and national level to propose new laws or to abolish contested regulations. All of these mechanisms make the political apparatus somewhat cumbersome, slowing the decision-making process.

As Switzerland has chosen to have a grass-roots parliament, so it has also chosen to have a grass-roots, militia-based army: all eligible men between the ages of 20 and

Geneva's cosmopolitan shopping district

36 are enrolled in the army and required to do regular military service. For, strange as it seems, neutral, peaceable Switzerland is ready to respond to any attack: anti-tank traps, bunkers and landing strips are hidden in the most bucolic valleys.

Executive power in Switzerland is entrusted to a cabinet of seven wise men and women, elected by the Parliament, in a system that respects the subtle balance of power among political parties, as well as among regions. These seven take it in turn to be President of the Confederation. Since each president's term only lasts one year, the average citizen often has a hard time remembering who is in office.

The modesty that characterises Switzerland's political figures extends to the population at large. The Swiss do not like to hear praise, either of their country's riches or of its position. Nonetheless, the average standard of living is high – and one must remember that this prosperity has been acquired in spite of meagre natural resources. Lacking coal and oil, the Swiss have struggled to tame the waters of their own Alps. Mineral resources are imported, then transformed into luxury goods that can be exported for profit.

CITY AND COUNTRY

The German-speaking majority occupies most of the country, except for the west and southwest. Zurich, the economic and financial capital, is at the heart of this majority. In the realm of international finance, the 'Zurich gnomes' have the reputation of being able to make judgments that can make or break a business, or several. But for tourists, the city offers elegant boutiques, museums, music and memories of a rich past. Geneva, the largest French-speaking city, has a very cosmopolitan air, thanks to its location at the French border and the presence of dozens of international businesses and organisations there. The political capital of the Swiss Confederation, Bern, is provincial and modest, lying halfway between these two linguistic poles and economic rivals. No grand monuments or majestic avenues here: Bern is too Swiss for such pomp. Nonetheless, it is one of the most agreeable capitals in Europe.

Each Swiss city has its own particular atmosphere, tied to its history, language and vocation. Even the smaller towns have much to offer culturally. Half a day by train is enough to go from the covered bridges of Lucerne to the orange groves of Lugano in the heart of the Italian region, but the spectacular change in language, culture and climate is as great as the Alps, which separate these two regions. Many Swiss villages deserve a stopover. Local arts and crafts, architecture (some small towns have remarkable medieval houses), local costumes– all offer something of interest, as does the landscape itself.

Unless you have made the trip just to visit museums and old country churches, you'll probably spend plenty of time outside, breathing the pure air of the mountains. If you have energy to

Rock climbing in St Moritz

spare, scale the peaks or explore them on a mountain bike or on foot – or try a via ferrata on a precipitous rock face; ski, windsurf, play tennis or golf; swim; go sailing, hang-gliding, waterskiing or fishing. Take a stroll in the country's plentiful woods, or the countryside, following the yellow-arrowed footpaths.

And the shopping... Shop windows tempt you with the most seductive luxury goods – watches, jewellery and the latest fashions. Given the quality of Swiss workmanship, these buys are worth considering. If your budget is tight, window-shop. Take time to stroll through the stalls of an open-air market; these are held once or twice a week in nearly every city and town, and you'll find flowers, fruit and vegetables in season, country bread and handmade objects.

In Switzerland you can eat well and with great variety, and there is something to suit every budget. The Geneva region, among others, is known for its extraordinary number of fine restaurants. Cheese is a favourite everywhere, in *raclettes* or fondues. Some regions, such as Valais, Neuchâtel or Ticino, are known for their wine-growing traditions. You can take a seat in the first café you see and try the local wine. No hurry: the locals often spend hours in such places, enjoying a *deci* (decilitre, or one-tenth of a litre) or a *demi* (half litre) of white wine, whilst relaxing and reading the newspaper.

A BRIEF HISTORY

Thousands of years before William Tell (see page 16), Switzerland was covered in glaciers. Its first-known inhabitants lived in caves, eking out a living by hunting and gathering. When the glaciers receded some 5,000 years ago, the people were able to move to the banks of lakes and rivers, where they built villages on pilings.

During the Second Iron Age, somewhere around 400 BC, a Celtic tribe known as the Helvetians, from whom Switzerland derives its original name, arrived in the region. In 58 BC, this tribe, looking for new territory, burned their farms and encampments and emigrated to the southwest. They are estimated to have numbered about 370,000 at that time. However, the legions of Julius Caesar stopped them at Bibracte, pushed them back and colonised their territory. The Romans established their administrative capital at Aventicum, nowadays just a village (Avenches) between Lausanne and Bern.

The Romans built roads and also brought in their technical developments and culture, just as later they would be the vehicle of the new Christian religion. During the decline of the Roman Empire, the eastern half of the country fell into the hands of the Alemanni, a warlike Germanic tribe, while the west came under the control of the Burgundians. The Sarine River, which marks the boundary between these two zones, remains to this day the linguistic and cultural frontier between German- and French-speaking Switzerland.

THE MIDDLE AGES

Both the Burgundians and the Alemanni were soon succeeded by the Franks, one of the most powerful Germanic tribes. Under Charlemagne (AD 768–814), the whole of what we now know as Switzerland was integrated into the Germanic Holy

Roman Empire. The abbeys that were to become centres of study and culture date from this era.

After the fall of the Carolingians in 911, a long period of political intrigue began, dominated by the powerful Zähringen and Habsburg families. In the mid-13th century, two powers emerged: the house of Savoy and the house of Habsburg. The inhabitants of central Switzerland opposed the extension of Habsburg influence, leading them to swear to a mutual assistance pact linking three valley communities, the *Waldstätten*: Uri, Schwyz and Unterwalden. This 'pact of defensive alliance', agreed upon at the beginning of August 1291, is considered to

THE WILLIAM TELL AFFAIR

In a country without kings, it is the people who make history. Whether William Tell is based on a legend or a real person, he nevertheless remains the Swiss national hero.

At the beginning of the 14th century, this simple peasant had the courage to stand up to a tyrannical governor. Having refused, in his passage through Altdorf, to salute the Bailiff Gessler, a representative of the Habsburgs, William Tell was condemned by Gessler to shoot an apple off his son's head with an arrow.

Tell succeeded in one try; when asked why he had taken two arrows from his quiver, he explained that the second was for Gessler, in case he missed his shot. Furious, the governor ordered him thrown in prison. Then, as he was being taken by boat to the castle dungeon, a storm hit the lake, the Vierwaldstättersee. Only Tell was able to keep the boat from being wrecked. He was untied and brought the boat ashore at a place now known as Tellsplatte, from which he managed to escape. Later, he led an ambush against the tyrant near Küssnacht and killed him.

Friedrich Schiller's play *William Tell* runs every summer to full houses in the open-air theatres of Interlaken and Altdorf.

be the foundation of the Swiss Confederation, an event commemorated every 1 August, Switzerland's national holiday. The legend of William Tell dates from around this period.

It was not until 1315 that the alliance took on its current meaning, when the Waldstätten fought the Habsburgs at the battle of Morgarten. The inhabitants of Schwyz fought so valiantly that the whole Confederation came to be called the 'Swiss'. During the 14th century, thanks to further alliances with other communities (Lucerne, Zurich, Glarus, Zug and Bern), the Confederation grew to eight cantons, all determined to fight foreign aggression.

Inside the William Tell chapel

The courage and prowess of the Swiss soldiers in the battles of Sempach (1386) and Näfels (1388), where they crushed the Habsburgs, contributed to forging a solid Swiss military reputation. This reputation was confirmed in the Burgundian wars (Grandson and Murten in 1476, Nancy in 1477).

TURN OF THE TIDE

The Battle of Marignano, in 1515, marked the first defeat of the Swiss army; more than 12,000 soldiers died in the battle. The Confederates nonetheless preserved their military reputation, henceforth serving as mercenaries to foreign armies. They no longer waged war on their own enemies, but rather on those of whoever paid them. The sight alone of these powerful halberdiers had a strong effect on their adversaries. It is their descendants who, today, stand guard at the Vatican in Renaissance costume. In 1516 the Confederation, which by then included 13 cantons (Fribourg, Solothurn, Basel, Schaffhausen and Appenzell had joined the alliance by this time), signed a perpetual peace treaty with France. Switzerland kept its territorial acquisitions (such as Ticino), while France won the right to requisition its mercenaries at any time.

RELIGIOUS STRIFE

The continual tensions of the 16th century were exacerbated by the Reformation. In 1522, five years after Martin Luther nailed his 95 theses to the Wittenberg church door in Germany, Ulrich Zwingli, a priest from Glarus who had become the preacher at the main church in Zurich, also defied papal authority. In the years to follow, Zurich, Bern, Basel and Schaffhausen would back the Reformation. But in the cantons of Uri, Schwyz, Unterwald, Lucerne and Zug, as well as in Solothurn and Fribourg, Catholicism remained firmly entrenched. Divided by religious zeal, the Confederation began to tear itself apart (the civil war of Kappel in 1531) before finally finding a compromise.

Ulrich Zwingli

Through the mediation of the French reformer Guillaume Farel, Bern encouraged the propagation of the Protestant Reformation in Neuchâtel and Geneva, and took advantage of its success to spread its influence further. Under constant threat from the Duke of Savoy, Geneva called on troops from Bern to defend itself. After chasing out the Savoyards, Bern occupied Vaud, where it worked to establish the new faith. But Geneva would not be dominated. In 1541, however, another French

Jean Calvin

reformer, Jean Calvin, managed to establish a Protestant theocracy in Geneva. The 'Protestant Rome' was born.

Lacking a centralised power and plagued by religious rivalries, the Confederates could not follow a coherent foreign policy. Since Marignano, they no longer participated in European conflicts except through their mercenaries. The Confederation embarked on the path of neutrality – an armed neutrality, born of the violation of Helvetian territory during the Thirty Years' War (1618–48). From 1647, this federal army, with Catholics and Protestants fighting side by side, watched over Swiss neutrality. Once peace was re-established in the treaty of Westphalia (1648), the Confederation was considered a sovereign state, its independence universally recognised. The canton of Bern played the most significant role.

From 1685 the country became a land of asylum for many French Protestants fleeing their homeland after the Revocation of the Edict of Nantes. But religious conflicts also raged in Switzerland throughout the 17th century. They broke

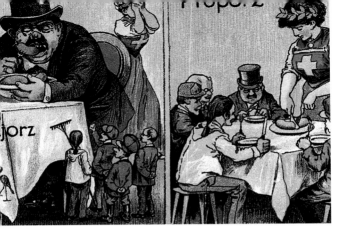

A 19th-century cartoon illustrating the campaign for proportional representation

out in 1656 (when victory went to the Catholics) and in 1712 (when the Protestants won the day), before ending in the Aarau peace agreement, which pronounced both religions equal. In the same period, social upheavals shook a Confederation where political rights still belonged only to the privileged. The profits of banking and commerce (in cotton, silk, wool and clock-making) remained in the hands of these few.

It is not surprising, then, that the repercussions of the French Revolution of 1789 were strongly felt in Switzerland. After having occupied or annexed the portions of the Confederation they wanted (in particular Basel, the cantons of Vaud, Valais, and Geneva), the revolutionary armies of France imposed the new Helvetic Republic, whose artificial, centralised structures were anathema to most Swiss citizens.

Napoleon Bonaparte put an end to three years of anarchy when he gave Switzerland a new constitution, the Act of Mediation (1803), inspired by the constitution of the ancient

Confederation, and added six new cantons to the 13 existing ones. He also took conscripts with him: 8,000 Swiss men died during the retreat of Napoleon's army from Russia.

NEUTRAL BUT CARING

The Congress of Vienna (1815) confirmed the independence and neutrality of Switzerland. Three new cantons (Valais, Geneva, which had been occupied by the French from 1798 to 1813, and Neuchâtel, which remained simultaneously under allegiance to Prussia until 1857) had just entered into the Confederation, giving the country its current geographic shape. But the religious struggles between Catholics and Protestants were reignited. In 1847, the Catholic cantons separated from the Confederation (the Sonderbund alliance); however, a campaign capably led by General Dufour ended three weeks later in the dissolution of the pact and imposed the return to peace. Political stability and national unity were assured in 1848 by a new constitution that established a true Swiss democracy, with power shared equally among communal, canton and federal authorities. The 1874 Constitution is still in effect today, and has preserved these foundations.

Internationally, Switzerland has been recognised since 1863, when Henri Dunant founded the Red Cross in Geneva. Since then, the country has offered asylum to many important refugees, from Lenin to Solzhenitsyn.

Geneva, headquarters of the League of Nations from 1920, has since become the European seat of the United Nations. Paradoxically, until 2002, Switzerland chose to remain outside the UN, for fear of threatening its neutrality.

This neutrality was harshly tested by two world wars. The first spared Switzerland but left it prey to a deep economic stagnation. As for the second, for 50 years the official line was that Switzerland had resisted entering the war thanks to its army and the will of its leaders and its people. In recent years, however, American investigators have uncovered the existence of Jewish funds confiscated by the Nazis during the war and deposited in Swiss bank accounts. In the aftershock of this discovery, the Swiss people are painfully having to rewrite their history.

It seems evident today that this small country, despite the real and courageous mobilisation of its army and people, could never have stood apart from the atrocities of the war without making certain compromises with the Nazi regime. Encircled for four years by Axis powers, Switzerland was forced to maintain most of its commercial relations with those countries. The leaders of that time had to make a choice between the preservation of the country and a morally irreproachable neutrality. Today, a more realistic and human vision is emerging: weaknesses and strengths coexisted here, as they did everywhere.

The concept of neutrality, along with that of direct democracy, remains at the heart of Switzerland's concerns, not only for historical reasons, but also for economic and political ones. However, in a change of heart after 50 years, the Swiss voted to join the UN in 2002. Yet isolation remains a feature of Swiss politics – only a year before voting yes to the UN, the Swiss rejected the opportunity to join the EU. Unconvinced of the benefits of joining the Union, for the moment the Swiss prefer to simply observe the coalition, while remaining at the heart of the continent.

Statue of Justice atop the Fountain of Justice in Bern

HISTORICAL LANDMARKS

58 BC Helvetians attempt to invade Gaul and are pushed back by Julius Caesar; Romans begin to colonise Swiss territory.

AD 260 First invasion of the Alemanni.

6th century Arrival of the Franks.

9th century Swiss territories incorporated into the Holy Roman Empire.

13th century Commercial importance of the 'Alpine corridor' grows.

1315 The Waldstätten crush Austrian troops at Morgarten; beginning of the military power of the Confederates.

1525 The beginning of the Reformation in Switzerland.

1536 The Confederation spreads to the French-speaking regions.

1685 Revocation of the Edict of Nantes; many Huguenots go into exile.

1798 France imposes a Republican structure on Switzerland.

1803 Return to federalism; six new cantons join the Confederation.

1815 Congress of Vienna consecrates Swiss independence and neutrality.

1847 The war of Sonderbund.

1863 Creation of the Red Cross in Geneva.

1914–18 Switzerland maintains its neutrality.

1937 Labour unions renounce the right to strike.

1939–45 Switzerland stays out of World War II.

1971 Swiss women win the right to vote in federal elections.

1979 French-speaking part of Jura secedes: birth of a 23rd canton.

1992 Referendum votes against joining European Economic Community, but for participation in the IMF and the World Bank.

2001 The Swiss vote to stay out of the European Union.

2002 Switzerland joins the United Nations.

2005 Swiss voters approve the Schengen Agreement, opening up the borders to citizens from other European countries.

2011 Switzerland announces plans to phase out nuclear power.

2016 The 57km (43-mile) -long Gotthard Base Tunnel, the longest in the world, opens to the public, connecting the cantons of Graubünden, Ticino and Uri together, via railway under the Alps

WHERE TO GO

Nothing could be easier than getting around Switzerland (see page 174). The motorway network is excellent, trains and buses service the most remote villages, and urban transport is extremely efficient.

This chapter contains some suggestions for trips within the country. They contain most of the important sites and should help you to plan your itinerary efficiently. The country has been divided into 12 regions that more or less correspond to those given by the Swiss tourist office.

Exploring more than one region a day is not impossible, but we don't recommend that you visit Switzerland at a racing pace. You will probably make your best discoveries off the beaten track. And don't forget that places that look close together on the map may not be so in reality. You may be overlooking the mountain ranges and hairpin turns that lie between one spot and the next.

ZURICH AND VICINITY

Greater Zurich (with 3.8 million inhabitants), at the extreme north of the lake of the same name, is Switzerland's largest urban centre. The city has been a major financial capital since its stock exchange was founded in 1877 but, despite its economic importance, the atmosphere of this town remains warm and human – earning it the nickname, the 'Big Small Town'.

The known history of **Zurich** ❶ (*Zürich*) goes back to the Neolithic period, when men built villages on piles along the banks of Lake Zurich (*Zürichsee*). Two thousand years ago, the Romans established a tax office, Turicum, for goods trafficked along the Limmat River. This spot, today known as

Limmat Riverside with the church tower of Sankt Peterskirche

Shopping in Bahnhofstrasse, Zurich's elegant retail hotspot

the Lindenhof, constitutes the geographic centre of the city. It took another thousand years for Zurich to be recognised as a city, and then to gain fame as a prosperous industrial centre specialising in silk, wool and linen weaving. In 1351, when Zurich joined the Confederation, its noblemen and merchants agreed to share their power with representatives from the tradesmen's guilds, whose guildhalls are still among the treasured monuments of the old town.

In the 16th century, Ulrich Zwingli brought the Reformation to Zurich, adding intellectual renown to the growing commercial and political importance of the city. Through the centuries, the city has distinguished itself as a centre of liberal ideas, attracting a number of great men, such as Goethe, Wagner, Thomas Mann, Einstein, James Joyce, Lenin and Trotsky (these last two spent innumerable hours together at Zurich's Café Odeon). It was from Zurich that Lenin and his Bolshevik colleagues departed, in 1917, aboard the famous 'sealed train' that crossed Germany to reach chaotic St Petersburg.

It was also in Zurich, at the Cabaret Voltaire on the Spiegelgasse, that the Dadaist art movement was born during World War I. Nowadays, the city has over 50 galleries exhibiting all kinds of artwork. The University of Zurich, Switzerland's largest, and the famous Federal Polytechnic (now the Swiss Federal Institute of Technology), considered one of the world's best engineering schools, set the intellectual tone for the city.

DISCOVERING ZURICH

The old town straddles the Limmat river, though the majority of its narrow, now pedestrianised, streets with small independent shops are on the east bank. The most elegant shopping street in Switzerland and one of the most prestigious in the world, the **Bahnhofstrasse Ⓐ** (1.5km/1 mile), connects the railway station to the lakefront. Jewellery, watches, haute couture, antiques and *objets d'art*: all the most luxurious items can be found here. Shaded by linden trees, the street is reserved for pedestrians, making it ideal for window-shopping. Not far from the station, one building will catch your eye: it's the observatory tower, the **Urania** (www.urania-sternwarte.ch; Thu–Sat 9–10.30pm), with the highest bar in the city. The observatory has a telescope with a magnification factor of 600.

The venerable **Fraumünster Ⓑ** (www.fraumuenster.ch/en; Jan–Feb 10am–5pm; Mar–Oct 10am–6pm; Nov–Dec 10am–4pm; free) dominates the west bank of the Limmat and overlooks the Münsterhof. There has been a church on this spot since a convent was founded here in 853. The current edifice dates from the 13th century and has a Romanesque choir with **stained-glass windows** designed by Marc Chagall.

On the Münsterhof, the **Zunfthaus zur Waag** dates from 1637; once home to the linen weavers' and hatmakers' guilds, it is now a restaurant, as are many old guild houses.

Chagall's glass

In 1967, at the age of 80, Marc Chagall began designing the famed stained-glass windows of the Fraumünster. Three years later they became one of Zurich's most visited attractions, and they still are today.

Charming little streets lined with boutiques and antiques shops lead you to the **Sankt Peterskirche** (Saint Peter's Church; www.st-peter-zh.ch; Mon–Fri 8am–6pm, Sat 10am–4pm, Sun 11am–5pm; free), the oldest church in Zurich. Its 13th-century bell tower houses one of the largest clocks in Europe, nearly 9m (30ft) in diameter. The baroque-style nave is decorated with pillars of pinkish-orange marble, delicate stucco and crystal chandeliers dating from the 18th century.

If you are willing to take on the steep stairs leading to the **Lindenhof**, you can enjoy a beautiful view over the Limmat, with its flat-roofed pleasure boats and the busy Limmatquai. This square's fountain was built in honour of the women of Zurich, who saved the city when it was besieged by the Habsburgs in 1292. Parading in full battle dress, they duped the enemy into believing that the city was too well defended to be conquered.

Wasserkirche, Sankt Peterskirche and Fraumünster

On the other side of the river, facing the Fraumünster, stands the cathedral, **Grossmünster** 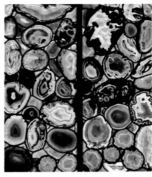 (www.grossmuenster.ch; Mar–Oct Mon–Sat 10am–5pm, Sun 12.30–5.30pm, Nov–Feb Mon–Sat 10am–4.30pm, Sun 12.30–4.30pm; free), built between 1100 and 1250 on the site of a 9th-century church. The Grossmünster is the uncontested 'mother church' of the Reformation in German-speaking Switzerland; Zwingli preached here from 1519

Stained glass by Giacometti in the Grossmünster

until his death in 1531. The stained-glass windows, designed by Augusto Giacometti, are a 20th-century addition. The twin towers, built in the 15th century and topped with domes from the 18th, are the city's most distinctive landmark. Windows by the same Giacometti also adorn the **Wasserkirche**, oddly situated astride the Limmat.

On the east bank of the river stand the ancient guild houses, each more splendid than the last: the **Zunfthaus zum Rüden**, one-time gathering-place of the nobility; the **Zunfthaus zur Zimmerleuten**, the house of the carpenters' guild, built in 1708 and decorated with oriel windows; and the **Zunfthaus zur Saffran**, headquarters of the haberdashers' guild. Opposite the latter is the **Rathaus** (Town Hall), dating from 1698. Zurich's municipal and cantonal parliaments still meet here.

After visiting the old town, take a stroll along the banks of the lake. The east side offers one surprising spot – the **Chinese Garden** (Mar–Oct Mon–Sun 11am–7pm), a gift to

Zurich from its twin city of Kunming. Birds, flowers, fish, streams and bridges – everything here has a flavour of the East. Along the lakefront, the **Zürichhorn** park has two wonderful attractions. The **Heidi Weber house** (www.centerle corbusier.com; July–Sept Sat–Sun 2–5pm), Le Corbusier's last work, is a refined mix of forms and colours. A little further, you'll find *Heureka* – a fantasmagoric extraterrestrial bird, created by sculptor Jean Tinguely. More recent developments include the shopping and leisure centre, Sihlcity, in an old paper factory; the opening of Schiffbau (shipyard) a collection of galleries and restaurants, and to the north of the centre in Viaduct is a 500-metre-long urban meeting place with independent shops and cafés under 36 arches.

ZURICH'S MUSEUMS

The **Kunsthaus** Ⓓ (Fine Arts Museum; www.kunsthaus.ch; Tue, Fri–Sun 10am–6pm, Wed–Thu 10am–8pm) contains collections of European painting from the Middle Ages to the 20th century, with Swiss artists particularly well represented. On view are works by Johann Heinrich Füssli, Arnold Böcklin and Ferdinand Hodler, both major figures of the 19th century, as well as the sculptor Alberto Giacometti. In addition to masterpieces by Monet, Cézanne, Van Gogh and Picasso, the museum possesses the largest collection outside Scandinavia of works by the Norwegian artist Edvard Munch.

One entire gallery is devoted to Marc Chagall, while another has Dadaist works by Hans Arp, Francis Picabia and Max Ernst. The museum owns collections from several important foundations, including the Alberto Giacometti Foundation, the Dada collection (with, most notably, the photographs of Man Ray) and the Swiss Photography Foundation.

The **Schweizerisches Landesmuseum** (Swiss National Museum; www.musee-suisse.ch; Tue–Sun 10am–5pm, Thu until 7pm), located in a curious Victorian-style edifice beside the Hauptbahnhof, celebrates the culture, art and history of Switzerland. Its halls are bursting with medieval sculpture and painting, and many rooms feature windows and frescoes that have been removed from ancient churches and houses and re-installed here. Upstairs, a huge room displays weapons, armour, uniforms and other military memorabilia. The museum also has reconstructed rooms from Swiss homes of several centuries ago.

Kunsthalle

Don't neglect the **Rietberg Museum** and Park Villa Rieter (www.rietberg.ch; Tue–Sun 10am–5pm, Wed until 8pm), tucked away in a luxurious exotic park. The museum contains traditional Chinese scroll paintings, Armenian carpets, Indian statues, Peruvian pottery, African masks and the like, all of which were assembled by the Baron von der Heydt.

The **Kunsthalle** (Museum of Contemporary Art; www.kunst hallezurich.ch; Tue, Wed, Fri 11am–6pm, Thu until 8pm, Sat–Sun 10am–5pm) shows international works in a 1,300 sq m (4,265 sq ft) exhibition space.

EXCURSIONS

For an amazing panoramic view of Zurich, its lake and the Alps, take the train up to **Uetliberg** (871m/2,860ft) from the

Collection Oskar Reinhart 'am Römerholz'

central train station or the Selnau station. The trip takes 20 minutes, and there is a train every half-hour.

To explore Zurich by the Limmat river, take one of the glass-topped boats that depart from the Landesmuseum every half-hour (from April to October) for a 50-minute tour. Cruises are also available to the **Zürichsee** (several options are available from Burkliplatz pier, ranging from 1 1/2 to 7 hours; lunch is provided on some trips) during which you can admire the lake-side villages surrounded by orchards, vineyards and appealing inns. The villages, especially those on the right bank (nick-named the 'Gold Coast'), make up Zurich's wealthier suburbs.

WINTERTHUR

Fifteen minutes from Zurich by road or train, **Winterthur** – known by the Swiss as Winti – is largely a commercial town, but it also has a graceful historic centre with plenty of green spaces, artistic monuments and buildings constructed between the 16th and 18th centuries. It is said that Winterthur is the town with the largest number of works of art per capita in the world. It owes this pre-eminence to the generosity of wealthy art patrons such as Oskar Reinhart, who left his collection to the town upon his death in 1965.

Half of the collection is displayed in a massive 19th-century building located in the middle of town. The **Museum Oskar Reinhart am Stadtgarten** (www.museumoskarreinhart.ch; Tue–Sun 10am–5pm) brings together some 500 choice works by Swiss, German and Austrian artists of the 18th, 19th and 20th centuries. Note in particular the rooms devoted to the work of the German landscape painter Caspar David Friedrich. And don't miss the portraits, landscapes and narrative paintings of Ferdinand Hodler. In the northern part of town, **Collection Oskar Reinhart 'Am Römerholz'** (www.roemerholz.ch; Tue–Sun 10am–5pm, Wed until 8pm), the villa where Reinhart himself lived, is home to the remainder of the collection; highlights include works by Cranach the Elder, Brueghel, Cézanne and Van Gogh.

Not far from the Reinhart Foundation, the **Kunstmuseum** (Fine Arts Museum; www.kmw.ch; Tue 10am–8pm, Wed–Sun 10am–5pm) shows interesting work by both Swiss artists (Füssli, Hodler, Vallotton) and French masters (Renoir, Rodin, Bonnard), as well as a superb Quentin Metsys, *Christ Giving His Blessing*.

At Oberwinterthur, northeast of the town, industry is the order of the day: **Technorama** (www.technorama.ch; daily 10am–5pm) showcases various aspects of technology, from household arts to industrial design, from the earliest motors to the latest computers.

Not to be missed is the **Fotomuseum Winterthur** (www.foto museum.ch; Tue–Sun 11am–6pm, Wed until 8pm), installed in an abandoned fabric factory and the first museum in German-speaking Switzerland to be devoted entirely to photography. It hosts five important touring exhibitions each year, and its reputation is still growing.

NORTHEAST SWITZERLAND

Commercial and industrial, but also with its fair share of natural beauty, this is one of the least celebrated areas of the country, often sidelined by tourists anxious to get to the household names further south. The region extends from Lake Constance (Bodensee) on the border with Germany to the peaks of the canton of Glarus to the south, encompassing the green and peaceful hills of the Appenzell in between.

SCHAFFHAUSEN

Industrial centre and communications nexus along the Rhine, **Schaffhausen** is the capital of Switzerland's northernmost canton, jutting into German territory like a lost puzzle piece. The heart of the old town, today a pedestrian zone, includes some of the most beautiful façades of the Swiss past.

Houses from the 16th, 17th and 18th centuries are adorned with statues, reliefs, sumptuous allegorical frescoes and richly sculpted oriel windows typical of this region. In 1570, Tobias Stimmer decorated the façade of the **Haus zum Ritter**, a house in the Vordergasse, with frescoes inspired by Roman myth and history. Note also, among the houses on the **Fronwagplatz**, the imposing **Grosses Haus**, which blends Gothic, baroque and rococo styles. The **Haus zum Goldenen Ochsen**, in the Vorstadt, is a Renaissance house noted for its sculpted decorations representing the five senses.

Chutes du Rhin

Heading down river from Schaffhausen, you arrive at the Chutes du Rhin (Rheinfall), the largest waterfall in Europe. Shuttles bring you here from town. With a volume of up to 1,080 cu m (240,000 gallons) every second, these falls are as impressive as they are noisy. Take a boat to the promontory, in the middle of the river, where you can feel the current's full force.

Chutes du Rhin (Rheinfall)

To the south, the 12th-century monastery of **Allerheiligen** (All Saints; www.allerheiligen.ch; Tue–Sun 11am–5pm) now houses a museum rich in illuminated manuscripts and incunabula.

The **Munot** (www.munot.ch; daily May–Sept 8am–8pm, Oct–Apr 9am–5pm; free), a vast circular fortress from the 16th century, dominates the town. From its dungeon, a spiral staircase allows access to the roof, from where there is a view of the town, the Rhine flowing through it and the surrounding vineyards.

Stein am Rhein, situated on the right bank of the river (19km/12 miles east of Schaffhausen), is a wonderful little town. Around the **market square** (Marktplatz) and in the small streets surrounding it, you can find frescoed, half-timbered houses with stepped gables and oriel windows. Some of these buildings date from the 16th century. Often, their decorations illustrate their names: House of the White Eagle, Inn of the Sun, House of the Red Ox and so on.

The **Kloster Sankt Georgen** (Convent of St George; www.bundesmuseen.ch; Apr–Oct Tue–Sun 10am–5pm), facing the town hall, was founded by Benedictines in the 11th century. Today, it is a museum of art and history. You can also visit the monks' cells, which have sculpted ceilings decorated with monochromatic frescoes.

The Baroque Stiftsbibliothek, St-Gallen's abbey Library

ST-GALLEN

Capital of lace and textiles, **St-Gallen** ❷ *(Sankt Gallen)* is located 85km (53 miles) from Zurich, between Lake Constance and the lower Alps of northeastern Switzerland. This dynamic city is an excellent example of the successful cohabitation of past and present, where medieval façades rub shoulders with modern buildings and trendy bars.

St-Gallen owes its name and existence to an Irish monk, Gallus, who settled here at the beginning of the 7th century. A hundred years later, a monastery was founded here in his memory, and a city soon sprang up around the abbey, with houses and artisans' workshops, a school and library. Here, monks practised the arts of manuscript illumination, poetry, and music, making St-Gallen a centre for Germanic culture.

In the old town, various abbatial buildings surround the **cathedral** *(Kathedrale)*, one of the last great baroque churches to be built in Europe (in the 1760s). Given the sobriety of the exterior, the white stucco and gold detailing of the interior are all the more striking.

The work these monks devoted themselves to 1,000 years ago is conserved at the **Stiftsbibliothek** (Abbey Library; www.stiftsbibliothek.ch; daily 10am–5pm), which occupies the west wing of the monastery buildings. Before entering, you will notice above the door the Greek inscription *psyche iatreion*, 'apothecary of the soul'. In this room, itself a treasure of baroque art, the shelves, which reach as high as the frescoed ceiling, contain some 100,000 volumes. The collection of manuscripts and incunabula – one of the richest in the world – comprises about 3,600 works. Manuscripts dating from the 9th to the 16th century are displayed in glass cases, the most precious being Irish, Carolingian and Ottonian illuminated manuscripts. To find your way around, look up at the cherubs over your head: they indicate the subjects of books in various parts of the room. For example, the cherub with his eye glued to a telescope is looking at the shelves devoted to astronomy.

APPENZELL

The geographic location and the customs of this region make it one of Switzerland's most traditional, a place that looks entirely like a picture-perfect Swiss postcard. The canton of Appenzell is divided into two parts: Inner Rhoden and Ausser Rhoden.

The cantonal seat of Inner Rhoden is **Appenzell ❸**,

Picture-postcard Appenzell

Appenzell cows

One of the best times to visit Appenzell is in late June and early July, when the farmers drive the cows up into the high Alpine pastures (Alpaufzug), or when they bring them back down again in late August or September. These are highly festive events: men in traditional red waistcoats and yellow breeches, wearing hats trimmed with edelweiss flowers, lead their herds of cows or goats, which are themselves decked out with cowbells and festive flowers.

a small town noted for its brightly painted wooden houses. In the souvenir stores, you can find handmade Appenzell embroideries, wooden buckets, cowbells, cheeses and naïve paintings by local farmer-artists. If you want to know more about regional art and history, it is worth heading to the **Appenzell Museum** (www.ai.ch; Mon–Wed, Fri 10am–12pm), located on the Hauptgasse.

Larger than Appenzell, **Herisau** is the cantonal seat of Ausser Rhoden; here you will also find a museum devoted to the history and craftsmanship of the region.

If the pastoral charm of this corner of paradise moves you, don't miss the picturesque villages of **Urnäsch**, **Gais** (known for its central square lined with 18th-century gabled houses) or **Trogen** with its own Landsgemeinde (open-air debate and vote), held every other year. In **Stein** you can also learn the secrets of Appenzell cheesemaking at the **Appenzeller Schaukäserei** (www.schaukaeserei.ch; Mar–Oct daily 9am–6.30pm, Nov–Feb Mon–Fri 9am–5.30pm; free).

The mountain of **Säntis** ❹ (2,503m/8,212ft) looms over this region. The roads leading to the mountain end at Schwägalp; from here, a cable car, in service year round, will take you to the top. Before your eyes spreads a panorama which extends from the Bernina range in the Grisons Alps, to Lake Constance.

NORTHWEST SWITZERLAND

Northwest Switzerland is the region encompassing the four German-speaking cantons of Basel-Stadt, Basel-Land, Solothurn and Aargau.

BASEL

The principal metropolis in northwest Switzerland, **Basel ❺** *(Bâle)* is the third-largest city in the country (pop. 189,000). It is also a major Rhine port, linking Switzerland with the sea; it is from here that Swiss exports begin their journey down the Rhine to Rotterdam. An international commercial crossroads, this great industrial centre is nonetheless quite charming thanks to parks, notable architecture and, as always, the river itself. Basel acquired its reputation as a great cultural centre as long ago as the 7th century. In 1033, the German emperor, Konrad II, captured the town from the Burgundians,

View from Kleinbasel onto the Mittlere Rheinbrücke

and Basel remained German until 1501, when it became the 11th member of the Swiss Confederation. In 1521, when the scholar Erasmus chose to teach here, the city (whose university, founded in 1460, is the country's oldest) became one of the great humanist centres north of the Alps.

Today, Basel is Zurich's rival for the title of Switzerland's richest city. Three hundred years ago, the bourgeoisie made its living in the silk trade; nowadays, the pharmaceutical and chemical industries are the primary sources of wealth. Each year, the Industrial Fair attracts more than a million visitors, and Basel's stock exchange is fast catching up with Zurich's.

EXPLORING THE CITY

Our tour begins at the **Mittlere Rheinbrücke** (Middle Bridge), where you can enjoy excellent views of the whole city, crowned by the cathedral and the magnificent medieval buildings that surround it.

Make your way into **Kleinbasel** (Little Basel): from the Oberer Rheinweg you have a splendid view of **Grossbasel** (Greater

FIFES AND DRUMS

The Basel Carnival (*Fasnacht*) is famous throughout Europe. It is a colourful three-day festival, with masks, drums and fifes, extraordinary costumes and giant lanterns. On the Monday after Ash Wednesday, at 4am, all the lights of the city go out; after a few impressive minutes of silence, lanterns are lit and, all over the city, the dance groups begin their march to the haunting rhythm of fifes and drums: this is the *Morgestraich*. While processions ebb and flow through the narrow streets, restaurants and cafés fill to the brim, politicians become fair game for satirists, and work and business take second place, or surrender completely.

Basel), which is older and more aristocratic than its smaller partner. Make a point of seeing the sculpture on the building at Schifflände 1, of the **Lälle-Keenig**, a medieval king sticking out his tongue. This is Grossbasel's way of showing its contempt for its little brother. But Little Basel gets to have its say on the Day of the Gryphon *(Vogel-Gryff)*, when the Wild Man *(Wilde Mann)*, riding by on a raft, climbs the bridge and does an insolent dance. This burlesque ceremony, every January, sets the tone for the riotous Carnival *(Fasnacht)* period.

Performers at Basel's carnival

Climb up the streets of Rheinsprung and Augustinergasse, lined with lovely old houses, to the **Münsterplatz**; this perfectly proportioned square is the site of a **Münster ⒶⒶ** (former cathedral; www.baslermuenster.ch; Easter–mid-Oct Mon–Fri 10am–5pm, Sat 10am–4pm, Sun 11.30–5pm, mid-Oct–Easter Mon–Sat 11am–4pm, Sun 11.30am–4pm; free) that has hardly changed since the 12th century. Note the detailing on the Gothic sculptures of the main portal. The main entrance used to be the Gallusporte, a beautiful Roman doorway. Inside, visitors stop to read the epitaph of Erasmus, who died in Basel in 1536.

The **Stadttheater** (Municipal Theatre) is a big modern building in the Theaterstrasse, facing a terraced square with a whimsical mechanical fountain, the **Fasnachtsbrunnen**,

Basel's 16th-century Rathaus

by Jean Tinguely. The latter is a humorous mixed-media construction, representing nine characters spitting into the water.

The three main commercial streets – Freiestrasse, Falknerstrasse and Gerbergasse – all lead to the **Marktplatz**, where you can mingle with the locals buying fruit, vegetables and flowers. On the square where the market is held stands one of the most striking buildings in all of Basel, the 16th-century **Rathaus** (town hall), adorned with small round turrets, larger towers, arches, Renaissance windows and a glittering gold steeple. The whole edifice, painted a vivid bright red, seems like a gigantic, surreal model – almost like a dolls' house.

In the 14th century, the citizens of Basel surrounded the city with a protective wall, of which just one jewel now remains: the **Spalentor**, the Western gate, topped by a clock tower and flanked by two crenellated guard towers. The sculptures of the Virgin and the prophets were added in the 15th century.

Children and grown-ups alike will appreciate the **Zoologischer Garten ❸** (Zoological Garden, or 'Zolli' for short; www.zoobasel.ch; daily May–Aug 8am–6.30pm, Mar, Apr, Sept and Oct 8am–6pm, Nov–Feb 8am–5.30pm), located southwest of town, not far from the railway station. With 4,000 animals of 600 different species on 13 hectares (32 acres) of land, it is the largest zoo in Switzerland. Founded more than a century ago, this serious institute of scientific study was the first zoo in Europe where gorillas, rhinoceros and other species reproduced in captivity.

BASEL'S MUSEUMS

Few museums in the world can rival the riches of the prestigious **Kunstmuseum ☉** (Fine Arts Museum; www.kunst museumbasel.ch; Tue–Sun 10am–6pm; Thu 10am–8pm). The first museum to open to the public in Europe, it is also the most well-attended museum in Basel. The Kunstmuseum contains the most comprehensive collection of Holbeins in the world, as well as works by the likes of Lucas Cranach, Matthias Grünewald, Konrad Witz, Martin Schongauer, Hans Baldung Grien, Albrecht Dürer and Rembrandt. The modern collections include works by Basel native Arnold Böcklin, Claude Monet, Paul Gauguin, Georges Braque, Max Ernst, Salvador Dali, Marc Chagall, Alberto Giacometti and Paul Klee, as well as a good number of Picasso's late works. Among the most popular pieces on display are those of Jean Tinguely, whose whimsical, fanciful creations delight both adults and children.

From the Kunstmuseum, it's just a 10-minute walk to the **Museum für Gegenwartskunst ☉** (Museum of Contemporary Art; www. kunstmuseumbasel.ch; Tue–Sun 11am–6pm, Thu 10am–8pm), which is located on the banks of the Rhine and housed in a converted paper mill. The main hall, lined with glass, houses Jonathan

Villa R, by Paul Klee

Borofsky's *Flying Man*, hanging at a third-floor height. The conceptual and minimalist creations of Frank Stella, Donald Judd, Carl André and Joseph Beuys stand in contrast to the extravagant new expressionism of Mimmo Paladino, Enzo Cucchi and Francesco Clemente. The new generation of Swiss artists is also well represented.

In the same contemporary spirit, the **Kunsthalle** (www.kunsthallebasel.ch; Tues–Fri 11am–6pm, Thu until 8.30pm, Sat–Sun 11am–5pm) has been presenting new names and trends in changing temporary exhibitions for more than a century.

In the Solitude park, a pastel-pink sandstone and glass building designed by Mario Botta houses the **Museum Tinguely** Ⓔ (www.tinguely.ch; Tue–Sun 11am–6pm). The collection brings together 35 years' worth of this artist's remarkable kinetic sculptures: note, in particular, the *Homage to New York* (1960) and Lola (1980).

The Museum Tinguely, which is filled with mechanical sculptures

The **Fondation Beyeler** (www.beyeler.com; daily 10am–6pm, Wed until 8pm), located in Riehen, contains a remarkable array of works. Among the artists represented here are Cézanne, Van Gogh, Monet, Picasso, Braque, Miró, Matisse, Mondrian, Kandinsky, Warhol, Rauschenberg and Lichtenstein.

EXCURSION FROM BASEL

To the east of Basel, **Augst**, the ancient town of Augusta Raurica, is sometimes called the 'Swiss Pompeii'. The 20,000 inhabitants of this flourishing Roman outpost (founded around 44 BC) enjoyed a theatre, temple, forum and baths, the ruins of which are still visible. A museum preserves all the artifacts found in digs at this site. In the summer, productions are mounted in the outdoor theatre (www.augst.ch; Mon–Fri 9am–11.30am, Mon, Fri 2pm–5pm; Wed 2pm–6pm).

SOLOTHURN

This small town is built on the Aare River, at the foot of the Jura range, around 65km (41 miles) south of Basel and 38km (24 miles) north of Bern. **Solothurn**'s past goes back to Roman times, but it is the baroque atmosphere that gives the town its special allure. In the 17th and 18th centuries, Solothurn *(Soleure)* the town, having resisted the Reformation, became the place of residence for ambassadors and envoys from Catholic France, who lived in fine patrician mansions.

The monumental **Sankt Ursenkathedrale** (Cathedral of St-Ursen) is built in a remarkable baroque Italian style. Its treasures include many precious relics, including the Hornbach Missal, an illuminated manuscript from the 10th century.

The **Altes Zeughaus** (Arsenal; www.museum-alteszeug haus.ch; Tue–Sat 1–5pm, Sun 10am–5pm), dating from the

15th century, is close to the main street (Hauptgasse). It contains a fine collection of arms and uniforms from the Middle Ages to the present day.

As you stroll down the Hauptgasse, you will see the **Jesuitenkirche** (Jesuit Church), a baroque building completed near the end of the 17th century. The best place to view the 12th-century **Zeitglockenturm** (clock tower) is from the terrace of a café on the market square. This astronomical clock, meticulously decorated with tiny figures, is over four centuries old.

Solothurn has many small town squares, each one with its own historic fountain. Notice the old houses with their heavy, overhanging roofs and dormer windows of a peculiar local design. Two medieval gateways, the Bieltor and the Baseltor, guard the entrance to the old town.

Beyond the fortifications, in the Werkhofstrasse, is the town's **Kunstmuseum** (Fine Arts Museum; www.kunstmuseum-so.

The 17th-century Baroque Jesuitenkirche in Solothurn

ch; Tue–Fri 11am–5pm, Sat–Sun 10am–5pm), which is worth a visit, if only to see the masterful *Madonna of Solothurn*, by Hans Holbein the Younger.

BADEN

Just 22km (14 miles) northwest of Zurich, **Baden** (literally, 'Baths') wears its name well. Two thousand years ago, the Romans were already taking dips in the hot springs of the *Aquae Helveticae* (Swiss waters). Today, visitors taking the waters enjoy luxurious surroundings in local hotels or municipal baths. Rich in mineral salts, these waters are recommended for the treatment of rheumatism, as well as neurological, respiratory and cardiovascular problems.

Begin your visit at one of the highest points in the town: the park facing the casino *(Kursaal)*, or the modern bridge spanning the Limmat river. From here, the view of the old town stretches out before you, down to the water.

Baden's **clock tower** *(Stadtturm)*, constructed in the late Gothic style, dominates the old town. The crenellated wall that climbs the hill connects the clock to a fortress, in ruins since the beginning of the 18th century.

Inside the 15th-century **Rathaus** is an historic room *(Tagsaztungssaal)*, where the representatives of the 13 original cantons met regularly between 1424 and 1712.

If you follow the ancient, winding streets back to the river, past a covered bridge dating from the 19th century, you will reach the **Landvogteischloss** (Bailiff's Castle; Tue–Sat 1–5pm, Thu 12pm–7pm; Sun 10am–5pm). Inside, a museum displays armaments and other artefacts from the canton of Aarau.

The Sydney and Jenny Brown galleries at the **Langmatt Collection** (Römerstrasse 30; www.langmatt.ch; Mar–Nov Tue–Fri 2–5pm, Sat–Sun 11am–5pm) feature a sizeable selection of Impressionist works.

Picturesque Bern, coated in snow

BERN AND VICINITY

The canton of Bern stretches from the French border in the northwest to the heights of the Alps in the south. Because of the diversity of the terrain, its towns and natural attractions, tourist authorities tend to divide it in two: the federal capital and the northern part of the region as one unit, and Interlaken and the alpine resorts – the Bernese Oberland – as another.

BERN

Bern ❻ *(Berne)* has been the capital of the Swiss Confederation since 1848 and with a population of 130,000 is one of Europe's smallest capitals. It is considered one of the best-preserved medieval cities on the continent and is listed by unesco as one of the world's cultural treasures. It is also one of the most 'blooming' towns in Europe: in addition to its many public gardens and forests, the façades and historic fountains are covered with flowers. The city, seat of the federal government and of numerous diplomatic offices, as well as various international organisations, remains an enclave of romantic calm.

Bern was founded in 1191 by Duke Berchtold V of Zähringen, who, looking for an impregnable bastion at the western frontier of his lands, decided to perch it on a rocky projection that was formed by a curve in the Aare river. In 1405, after a fire that destroyed nearly all its wooden houses, Bern was rebuilt in sandstone.

In 1353, after fighting the Habsburgs to defend its independence and freedom, Bern joined the Confederation. The expansion of its holdings to the west brought the French-speaking regions into the Confederation. In 1848, Bern was chosen to be the seat of the federal government.

THE OLD TOWN

Begin your exploration of Bern at the railway station: you will discover that the underground shopping galleries here contain the remains of the Christoffelturm (Saint Christopher Tower), part of the old city ramparts.

Take the escalator to street level, to emerge at the start of a lively shopping street, the **Spitalgasse**, where major department stores hide behind elegant old façades. Most of the streets of the old town are edged by covered arcades, making up a promenade 6km (4 miles) long. Under the arcades, you can stroll peaceably in any weather, enjoying the musicians and street artists along the way.

The Bern bear

The bear representing the Zähringen family is everywhere: in statue form, on the flag and even alive and well in the Bear Pit (see page 52). Legend has it that when Duke Berchtold V decided to build the city, he swore to name it after the first animal he brought back from the hunt; that animal turned out to be a bear (*Bär*, in German).

The Zeitglockenturm

Bern is full of **fountains**, most of them dating from the 16th century. Their columns generally support allegorical figures painted in bright colours. The first one you will come across is the Pfeiferbrunnen (Bagpiper Fountain), which is probably the work of Hans Gieng, who designed many of these attractive local landmarks.

Further down Spitalgasse lies the **Käfigturm** (17th century) which was once a watchtower, later a prison. Turn left into Waisenhausplatz, where you will see the Waisenhaus (orphanage), a beautiful 18th-century building. The modern fountain nearby, designed by Meret Oppenheim, is a controversial addition. South of the Käfigturm, the Bärenplatz, home to cafés and giant open-air chessboards, is always lively.

Two more fine fountains can be found on **Marktgasse** (return to the Käfigturm and turn right): one is an allegory of *Temperance* – a woman diluting wine with water, in homage to Anna Seiler, founder of the Island Hospital, who donated her house to take in victims of epidemics – while the other, the Schützenbrunnen (Arquebusier Fountain), is decorated with a flag-bearer. Local legend claims that the ogre-topped **Kindlifresserbrunnen**, on the Kornhausplatz (to your left at the end of the Marktgasse), was built to scare children. The **Kornhaus**, once a grain depository, is now a cultural centre hosting exhibitions and other events. This group of buildings also includes the Fine Arts and Industrial Arts libraries. Don't hesitate to take a seat in the Kornhaus Café, a successful combination of ancient walls and modern touches.

The **Zeitglockenturm** Ⓐ (clock tower), the oldest monument in Bern, is so unusual you might want to organise your visit around it, so you can witness this extraordinary display of 16th-century Swiss clockwork. Try to arrive at least five minutes before the hour and prepare to take in the show: a jester contorts himself to ring two bells above his head, a procession of bears follows, a rooster crows and flaps his wings, Father Time turns over his hourglass, and so on.

Beyond the Zeitglockenturm, on **Kramgasse**, the Zähringerbrunnen (Zähringen Fountain) is topped by a bear in armour, with a baby bear at his feet. The *Mutz*, as Bern natives have nicknamed him, was built in honour of the city's founder. Albert Einstein and his family lived from 1902 to 1909 at number 49 on Kramgasse. The apartment where the physicist developed his theory of relativity has been converted into a small museum.

Located further down Kramgasse, and one street to the left, is the **Rathaus**, a ravishing Gothic construction that

$E = MC2$

In 1905, while working at the Swiss Patent Office in Bern, a young Albert Einstein spent much time thinking about a multitude of theories concerning light, space and time. It was in this year, called the Annus Mirabilis (Miracle Year), that Einstein developed the Special Theory of Relativity, or E=mc2. He spent most of his time working on this theory and several others, including his Nobel Prize-winning theory on light quantum, at Kramgasse 49, where he lived with his wife and son for several years. A small museum is located here. It is believed that Einstein thought often about Bern's famous Zeitglockenturm to relate light and time as he developed his famous theory.

rises up between Postgasse and Postgasshalde. Note also the colourful Vennerbrunnen (Flagbearer Fountain), which shows a Bernese standard-bearer in full uniform. As you continue along Kramgasse into Gerechtigkeitsgasse the **Gerechtigkeitsbrunnen** fountain represents the allegory of Justice. At the end of the street, you will be faced with two tempting choices: you can cross the bridge and go straight to the Bear Pit, or take a left on the Nydeggstalden to the oldest part of town. After the Nydeggkirche (Nydegg Church), head down to the Läuferplatz to see the **Untertorbrücke**, the oldest bridge in Bern (1461–89). To the left, the Läuferbrunnen (Messenger Fountain) pays homage to a herald from Bern who, reproached by the king of France for not speaking French, had the audacity to reply: 'Well, you can't speak German!'

To get to the recently enlarged **Bear Pit Ⓑ** *(Bärengraben)*, turn right after the Untertorbrücke and follow the ramp. Bern without its bears would be like Paris without the Eiffel Tower. Bears have enjoyed pride of place here since the 15th century – with the exception of the period of French occupation, during which time the mascots were confiscated. The crowd is at its most dense on Easter morning, when, if weather permits, the mother bears and their new cubs are brought out for the first time each year.

Kramgasse near Zähringen fountain

Cross back over the Nydeggbrücke and walk up the Junkerngasse to the **Münster Ⓒ** (www.bernermuenster.ch; winter Mon–Fri noon–4pm, Sat 10am–5pm, Sun 11.30–4pm; summer Mon–Sat 10am–5pm, Sun 11.30am–5pm; free), Switzerland's most majestic cathedral built in the late Gothic style. It took more than two centuries to complete. The nave, begun in 1421, was only finished 150 years later, and not until 1893 was the openwork spire, 100m (328ft) high, added. The largest of the bells, weighing more than 10 tonnes, was installed in 1611. *The Last Judgement* (1490–95, on the tympanum over the main entrance), a remarkable work by Erhart Küng, represents a series of 234 damned and chosen souls, recruited from every social class. In the choir, the beautiful 15th-

Münster Cathedral

century **stained-glass windows** illustrate, in particular, the three kings and an impressive *danse macabre*; don't miss the magnificent Renaissance **choir stalls**. A staircase leads to the second terrace of the tower, with a splendid view of the city.

From the **Münsterplattform**, an incredible lift takes you to the riverbank, in the old popular neighbourhood of **Matte**. Now renovated, the district is full of boutiques, crafts stands and artists' studios, and makes for a very agreeable walk. Near the Münsterplattform, the **Bundeshaus** Ⓓ (Federal Parliament Building), built in the 19th century, is the seat of Swiss government. Guided 45-minute tours are available most of the year; check times on www.berninfo.com and remember to take your passport. Pre-booking is advisable at busy times.

Climb the Gurten

For a brief excursion, you can climb the Gurten (858m/2,185ft high), where the view of Bern and the surrounding Alps is just extraordinary. It takes about 25 minutes to get to the summit by tramway (the number 9 line), then on the funicular running out of Wabern, just south of the city centre.

BERN'S MUSEUMS

The **Kunstmuseum** Ⓔ (Fine Arts Museum; www.kunst museumbern.ch; Wed–Sun 10am–5pm, Tue 10am–9pm), at Hodlerstrasse 12, displays examples of Bernese painting from the Middle Ages to 19th-century Realism as well as a rich collection of modern art with works by Manet, Cézanne, Monet, Renoir, van Gogh and Hodler. There are also works by Paul Klee, who was born in Bern and died here in 1940. Most of the Klee collection, however, has been moved to the **Zentrum Paul Klee** (www.zpk.org; Tue–Sun 10am–5pm), 10 minutes by bus or tram from Bern's old town. This museum, which is devoted solely to Klee's work, has around 4,000 paintings.

The **Kunsthalle** (Art Institute; www.kunsthalle-bern. ch; Tue–Fri 11am–6pm, Sat–Sun 10am–6pm), located at Helvetiaplatz 1, is devoted to contemporary art and stages temporary exhibitions of avant-garde works.

Mountain-lovers will rush to the **Schweizerisches Alpines Museum** (Swiss Alpine Museum; www.alpines museum.ch; Tue 10am–8pm, Wed–Sun 10am–5pm), at Helvetiaplatz 4, where topographic reliefs of the mountains and other maps are on display alongside antique skiing and climbing equipment.

The **Museum Für Kommunikation** (Museum of Communication; www.mfk.ch; Tue–Sun 10am–5pm), at Helvetia Strasse 16, tells the story of the postal service, the telegraph and the telephone, from the earliest centralised phones to the most modern teleprinters. Rare stamps, both Swiss and foreign, are on display in the basement.

The **Bernisches Historisches Museum** (Bern Historical Museum; www.bhm.ch; Tue–Sun 10am–5pm), in an extraordinary neo-Gothic building at Helvetiaplatz 5, contains artisanal objects as well as armaments, figures and jewellery. Its most precious possession is the booty seized from the Duke of Burgundy in the battle of Grandson (1476), including battle standards, manuscripts and precious tapestries. An exhibition dedicated to Einstein was recently added.

The collections of the **Naturhistorisches Museum** (Museum of Natural History; www.nmbe.ch; Mon 2–5pm, Tue, Thu and Fri 9am–5pm, Wed 9am–6pm, Sat–Sun 10am–5pm), at Bernastrasse 15 figure among the richest in Europe. Zoology, geology, mineralogy and palaeontology are particularly well represented and well displayed.

Zentrum Paul Klee

BIEL

Prehistory and modern industry live side by side in **Biel** *(Bienne)*, a town of rivers, streams and canals, situated on the lake of the same name about 32km/20 miles northwest of Bern. Its many watchmaking firms give it its nickname, the 'Swiss watch capital'. The town gets its particular character from the bilingual meeting of two cultures (two-thirds of the population speak Swiss German, one-third speak French). The Biennese juggle the two languages without confusion.

The medieval old town is perfect for a leisurely stroll, particularly beneath the arcades of the **Obergasse**. Here, as in Bern, the 16th-century fountains draw the visitor's gaze with their boldly coloured statues. Notice the Vennerbrunnen (Flagbearer Fountain), on the **Ring**, a central plaza surrounded by an impressive architectural ensemble.

The Biennese take their prehistory to heart. It was a native of Biel, Friedrich Schwab (1803–69), who discovered at La Tène (on Lake Neuchâtel) the vestiges of a second Iron Age culture. The objects he excavated belonged to the ancient civilisation known as La Tène and are now on display in the Biel museum named after Schwab.

From Biel, it takes approximately an hour and a half to walk out to the **Taubenloch gorges** (Taubenlochschlucht). A footpath leads to this site of wild beauty, which is known as the gateway to the Jura Mountains. **Evilard**, a little village perched on the hills above Biel, offers a marvellous view of the high peaks in the Bernese Oberland lying beyond Bern.

In about 50 minutes, a boat will take you to **St Peter's Island** *(Sankt Peterinsel)*, on Lake Biel. This nature preserve is an island only in name, since drainage lowered the water level during the 19th century, turning St Peter's into a peninsula connected to the mainland. In the 18th century, St Peter's Island so captivated that 'friend of nature' Jean-Jacques Rousseau that he stayed here from 1765 to 1767. The hotel room where the philosopher lived, full of mementos, still attracts nostalgic visitors.

THE EMMENTAL

Everything about Switzerland that is rural, green, peaceful and perfectly clean is encapsulated by the **Emmental**. Even the most urban visitor will soon admit that the natural beauty of this region is impossible to resist.

Just 22km (14 miles) northeast of Bern, **Burgdorf** *(Berthoud)*, which overlooks the Emmental Valley, is a centre for the textile industry. The restored 12th-century castle has a small museum of local history. From Burgdorf, a pretty road follows the valley of the River Emme to the fair-sized village of **Langnau**, some 30km (19 miles) from Bern. Besides its interesting folk museum, Langnau offers an excellent sweet cheese studded with large holes – the delicious Emmental.

A bike ride in the Emmental Valley

BERNESE OBERLAND

The Oberland, lying to the south of Bern, is a region with much to offer the tourist: majestic mountains, impressive glaciers, vast lakes and cascades, charming villages, and well-equipped holiday resorts. Since the beginning of the 19th century, well before skiing and hiking became popular pursuits, the English and French elite came here to relax in luxury hotels and to see, far off, the peak of the Jungfrau. Some of them even ventured as far as the glaciers.

AROUND LAKE THUN

Thun *(Thoune)*, tucked into the northernmost edge of the lake of the same name, occupies a remarkable site: the centre of the old town sits on a long, narrow island on the Aare, just where the river flows out of the lake. This island, small enough to cross easily on foot, is linked to dry land by several bridges. Thun's main commercial street, the **Hauptgasse**, is curiously built on two levels, so that you walk on top of the flower-bedecked roofs of the stores that line it, while admiring the windows of a second level of boutiques.

At the end of the street, between numbers 55 and 57, take the covered staircase leading to the castle and the baroque parish church.

The breathtaking Bernese Alps

The **Schloss Thun** is a group of fortifications crowned by a Romanesque tower topped with a smaller tower at each corner. The **Historisches Museum** (Historical Museum; www.schlossthun.ch; daily Apr–Oct 10am–5pm, Nov–Mar 1–4pm), founded in 1888, occupies five storeys of the tower. The main room is the Knights' Room, a majestic chamber hung with 15th-century tapestries, with pikes and halberds on display. On the floor above are Swiss military uniforms and armaments from the ancient crossbow to modern-day weapons. On the floor below, you will find artisanal works and a collection of toys.

The pyramid-like silhoutte of the Niesen on Lake Thun

A paddlesteamer and more modern ships ply Lake Thun, offering pleasant excursions. Along the north bank, a road leads from the lake to the hills, ending at **Oberhofen**. This village is known for its medieval castle, which was reconstructed and sumptuously decorated during the 17th and the 19th centuries and now houses a section of the Bern Historical Museum.

On the south bank of the lake, the town of **Spiez** also has an imposing castle dating from the 12th and 13th centuries. Don't miss the magnificent panoramic view from the **Niesen** (2,336m/7,664ft), an impressive natural pyramid. To reach the top, take the funicular from Mülenen, about 2km (1 mile) south of Spiez.

Several ski resorts can be conveniently reached from Spiez. If you take the train or road through the Simmental, you will reach **Gstaad** ❼, a resort that has long been fashionable with the world's rich and famous, who come here to ski and be seen in an atmosphere that's decidedly chic and in surroundings of great natural beauty.

INTERLAKEN

The famous ski centre of **Interlaken ❽** is located, as its name indicates, between the lakes of Thun and Brienz, and offers a splendid view of the Jungfrau mountain, with its perpetual cloak of snow.

Höheweg (or Höhe), a magnificent boulevard shaded by trees, offers gorgeous views of the surrounding peaks. The north side is occupied by grand Victorian-era hotels, restaurants, boutiques and the famous casino *(Kursaal)*. The sunnier and more open southern part features a beautiful park, the **Höhematte**, with a view that opens on to the Jungfrau. You can travel around Interlaken by horse-and-carriage or on foot, or escape the crowds on a hiking trail. From Wilderswil, 2km (1 mile) away, a cog railway climbs up to the **Schynige Platte**. As well as a superb panorama of the Bernese Alps, this site offers visitors a garden of alpine blooms.

TOWARDS THE PEAKS

Train enthusiasts and armchair alpinists will find it hard to resist the attraction of a comfortable journey from Interlaken to Jungfraujoch, the highest railway station in Europe (3,454m/11,332ft). In clear weather, the spectacle is one of a kind, and the air is extraordinarily pure.

From Interlaken, you can make part of the journey by car to **Grindelwald** (a lively international ski resort) or **Lauterbrunnen**. From either place, the train will take you

St Beatus Caves

Just outside Interlaken on the east bank of Lake Thun lies the natural wonder of the St Beatus Cave carved into the Niederhorn massif. A kilometre (1/2mile) of caves can be toured by well-lit paths. Guided tours depart every 45 minutes. There is also a small museum and restaurant on-site (www.beatushoehlen.ch; mid-Mar–Oct daily 11.30am–5.30pm).

to the Jungfrau, but it is easier and more enjoyable to make the whole journey by train. The construction of this railway – the **Jungfraubahn** (www.jungfraubahn.ch) – was one of the great technological achievements of the end of the 19th century. It tunnels through hard rock for 7km (4½ miles) to reach Europe's highest station.

Whether you come from Grindelwald or Lauterbrunnen, you will reach the Jungfraubahn at the **Kleine Scheidegg** (Little Scheidegg) station, at the foot of the awe-inspiring North Wall of the **Eiger**, first conquered in 1938. The mountain is surrounded by the soaring peaks of the **Wetterhorn**, the **Mönch** and the **Jungfrau** (4,158m/13,642ft).

COGS AND CABLE CARS

You can climb a Swiss mountain the hard way, with crampons, a pick and some rope. But an easier method of accessing the pure air of the peaks is to take advantage of technology – technology that, in Switzerland, is breaking records by leaps and bounds.

Since the end of the 19th century, the cog-wheel railways have made communications possible over the mountains. The Viznau-RigiBahn, finished in 1871 by the Swiss engineer Riggenbach, is the oldest cog train in Europe. The Pilatus (Lucerne), which travels on the world's steepest tracks (48°) has been running since 1889. In Zermatt, one of these trains goes as high as Gornergrat (3,130m/10,270ft). Finally, the highest train in Europe climbs to Jungfraujoch, at an altitude of 3,454m (11,332ft).

Cable cars often pick up the next leg of the climb, easily crossing the most difficult zones. The highest line in Europe links Zermatt to the Matterhorn, at more than 3,800m (12,467ft).

Saas-Fee has an Alpine subway, which goes from the Felskinn cable car stop (3,000m/9,838ft) to Mittelallalin (3,500m/11,483ft). Not surprisingly, the Metro Alpin is the highest subway in the world.

The train then enters an almost continuous series of tunnels after the Eigergletscher station, where the Eiger glacier looms into view. It also briefly stops at Eigerwand (the Wall of Eiger) and Eismeer (the Ice Sea), for passengers to get out for a glimpse of the marvellous view through the 'picture windows' carved in the rock.

Jungfraubahn and the Eiger

The last station is **Jungfraujoch** ❾, where a restaurant and observation terrace dominate the Aletschgletscher, the longest of the Alpine glaciers at 25km (15 miles). Dress warmly, even in summer, and wear appropriate shoes: if weather permits, you can go for a walk (but stay inside the signposted safe areas) or take a ride in a dogsled. The ice sculptures on view at the 'Ice Palace', as well as a small exhibition on scientific research at high altitudes, are worth a look.

Another excursion to undertake in good weather is a trip to the **Schilthorn** mountain, which offers a fine view of the Alps. From Stechelberg and **Mürren** ❿ (a romantic village completely without cars, perched on a veritable 'balcony' facing the Eiger, Mönch and Jungfrau mountains), a cable car (www.schilthorn.ch) climbs to a height of 2,970m (9,744ft) to leave you at the Piz Gloria revolving restaurant (made famous by the James Bond movie *On Her Majesty's Secret Service*). It takes 50 minutes for the turning platform to complete one rotation, allowing plenty of time for gazing out over the Bernese Alps, Mont Blanc and the Jura and Vosges mountain ranges.

Don't leave this region without having seen the **Trümmelbach Waterfalls** (3km/2 miles from Stechelberg). A lift takes you to the well-lit galleries, where the impressive cascades burst from underground gorges. Don't forget your raincoat.

BRIENZ LAKE

A small blue marvel with wilder and more dramatic surroundings than those of its brother, Lake Thun, the Brienzersee is linked to the Thun by the Aare River.

The town of **Brienz**, towards the eastern end of the lake, is the Swiss capital of wooden sculpture. The town also has a school of wood sculpture, another for the handcrafting of string instruments and several souvenir stores.

The **Brienzer Rothorn** looms over the region from its height of 2,351m (7,713ft). The hour-long journey up the Rothorn, in an old-fashioned railway carriage pushed by a steam engine, reveals scenes of tranquil, breathtaking beauty (www.brienz-rothorn-bahn.ch). Another popular excursion begins with a boat ride to the wooded bank of the lake facing Brienz; then, from Giessbach See, a funicular transports travellers to the **Giessbach Falls**, a superb series of waterfalls, which hurtle straight down 400m (1,312ft). Simply one of the most romantic spots imaginable, Giessbach is home to an old hotel that has been beautifully renovated.

Many villages and market towns of the Oberland have a church, a town hall and a folklore museum. None, however, is as ambitious as the **Open-Air Museum of Ballenberg** ⓫ (www.ballenberg.ch; mid-Apr–Oct daily 10am–5pm), about 2km (1 mile) northeast of Brienz on the route to Brünig, with regular buses from Brienz station. The 'Ballenberg' groups together village houses, some more than three centuries old, brought here from all over the country. Seeing them together underlines the great variety of styles, materials and methods in Swiss construction: the Oberland chalet, for example, with its low roof and highly wrought façade, is very different from the typical house of central Switzerland, in wood and masonry. The interiors are authentically furnished, and the houses have vegetable plots in their back gardens and farm animals. Here and there, artisans demonstrate their craft according to traditional methods.

The Trift Suspension Bridge

Meiringen, a pretty little town 20km (12 miles) from Brienz, on the upper banks of the Aare (Haslital), is popular with excursionists and alpinists. Fires in the 19th century destroyed most of the historic buildings, but some wooden constructions typical of the region were saved.

The hike to the **Trift Suspension Bridge**, just east of Meiringen, is a unique high-mountain experience. The rope bridge, which overlooks Lake Trift and the Trift Glacier, is one of the longest of its kind in Europe. Reaching it requires a 10 minute cable car ride (starting from Oberhasli; open July–Sept) and a challenging, vertiginous 90-minute hike, each way.

While you're in the area, you should try to see the deep **Aare Gorge** *(Aareschlucht)*, a striking natural attraction at the foot of the Susten and Grimsel mountain passes. Assiduous readers of Sir Arthur Conan Doyle won't want to miss the nearby **Reichenbach Falls** ⑫, reached by funicular (www.

reichenbachfall.ch). It is here that Sherlock Holmes and his arch-enemy Moriarty plunged together to their deaths. The famous detective later had to be resuscitated, under pressure from readers hungry for new adventures.

LUCERNE AND CENTRAL SWITZERLAND

Here, you are in the land of William Tell, at both the historical and geographical heart of the country. Travellers have been attracted to this lush region since long before the age of tourism. This area includes the cantons of Lucerne, Zug, Uri, Nidwalden and Obwalden.

LUCERNE

Just about all the elements of a perfect tourist town converge in **Lucerne** 🔞 (*Luzern* in German): a splendid waterfront setting against a backdrop of mountains; historic churches, interesting shops, and plenty of greenery; several outstanding annual music festivals and a fine fleet of paddlesteamers.

A thousand years ago, Lucerne was a humble fishing village that happened also to be home to a Benedictine monastery. Under the domination of the powerful Alsatian Abbey of Murbach, it became a merchant city; its importance increased with the opening of the St Gotthard pilgrimage route. Citizens of Lucerne enjoyed relative freedom until 1291, the year the Habsburgs took the city. To release itself from their control, Lucerne turned in 1332 to the young Swiss Confederation. After the victory of the Confederates at the battle of Sempach in 1386, Lucerne, now independent, enjoyed a period of prosperity. A Catholic bastion, it remained resistant to the Reformation.

Secret capital

Many consider Lucerne to be the secret capital of Switzerland: if Bern is the head, and Zurich the hand, then Lucerne can certainly pride itself on being the heart of the country.

By the 18th century, Lucerne was the country's biggest town and also the centre of Catholic Switzerland. In 1847, while the Catholic cantons were seceding from the Confederation, Lucerne placed itself at the head of the rebellion. After the reconciliation, grand hotels were built along the lake; in 1870, the legendary César Ritz opened the Grand Hotel National. Alexander Dumas defined Lucerne as 'a pearl in the world's most beautiful oyster'.

Lucerne – the Reuss river in front of the Jesuit church

THE OLD TOWN

The very model of the Swiss covered bridge, the **Kapellbrücke** (Chapel Bridge), a symbol of Lucerne, was built at the beginning of the 14th century over the Reuss river. It burned down in 1993 – an emotional shock for Lucerners – and was reopened in 1994. Copies of over 100 paintings dating from the 17th century adorn the triangles formed by its ceiling beams, telling the story of the patron saints of the city and of heroes of Lucerne, as well as depicting episodes from Swiss history. The bridge can only be crossed on foot. Until the 19th century the octagonal stone tower alongside it, the **Wasserturm** (Water Tower), was used as a prison, an archival library and a treasury.

A little further along the left bank of the river, the **Jesuitenkirche** (Jesuit Church), begun at the end of the 17th century, is one of the oldest and most beautiful baroque buildings in Switzerland. Its pink-and-white interior, decorated with stucco and frescoes, dates from 1750, while the towers are from 1893. Follow the Bahnhofstrasse away from the banks of the Reuss to reach the **Franziskanerkirche** (Franciscan Church), built in the 13th century in the Gothic style.

Return to the river and follow its course past the Zeughaus, the old arsenal, to cross the **Spreuerbrücke** (Mill Bridge). This covered wooden bridge from the early 15th century is decorated with superb artworks painted between 1625 and 1632. Their theme, a common one in the Middle Ages, is the dance of death.

On the right bank, you enter the most striking part of the city: the **Weinmarkt** (Winemarket Square), the heart of medieval Lucerne. Most of the buildings that encircle it – old guild houses, boutiques and patrician homes – have

Snow covering Lucerne's old town and Chapel Bridge

preserved their elaborately painted façades. Particularly worth a look is the Weinmarktapotheke (Winemarket Pharmacy), built in 1530. Nearby, the **Hirschenplatz** (Deer Square), also surrounded by old houses, used to host the city's hog market.

The houses of the nobility around the **Rathaus** (town hall) are joined by several floors of arcades. One of these houses, the beautiful Haus Am Rhyn, at Furrengasse 21, is home to a fascinating collection of Picasso's late works and 200 photos of the painter by the photographer David Douglas Duncan; however, it is currently closed to visitors. Not far away, the **Rosengart Collection** (www.rosengart.ch; daily Apr–Oct 10am–6pm, Nov–Mar 11am–5pm), at Pilatusstrasse 10, has many works by Picasso, as well as several works of Klee, Monet, Renoir and Cézanne among others.

Turning from the Reuss, walk up to the **Museggmauer**, part of the longest (at 870m/2,854ft) and best-preserved for-tified city walls in Europe. From Easter to October, a section of these 600-year-old ramparts and three of its towers are open to the public. On the **Zyt Tower**, the oldest clock in town (dating from 1535) chimes one minute before every hour.

A short walk takes you past the Museumplatz and the Löwenplatz to **Löwendenkmal** (the Lion monument). What Mark Twain called 'the most lugubrious and moving block of stone on earth' is dedicated to the memory of 800 Swiss mer-cenaries who died during the French Revolution, in particular in the Tuileries on 10 August 1792, while defending King Louis XVI and his family. This lion, mortally wounded with a blow of the lance, was carved in stone in 1821, after a drawing by the Danish sculptor Bertel Thorvaldsen.

Alongside the lion, you can see the 'giants' tureens' in the **Gletschergarten** (Glacier Garden; www. gletschergarten.ch; daily Apr–Oct 9am–6pm, Nov–Mar 10am–5pm). These are deep potholes created 20,000 years ago by the glacier that covered this region. To better understand this geological phenomenon, go to the park museum, where fossils and minerals are on display.

Also nearby, the **Bourbaki Panorama** (www.bourbaki panorama.ch; Apr–Oct daily 9am–6pm, Nov–Mar daily 10am–5pm), a gigantic round painting illustrating the entry into Switzerland of French troops commanded by General Bourbaki after their defeat at the hands of the Prussians (January 1871), stands 10m (33ft) tall and 114m (375ft) wide.

The **Verkehrshaus der Schweiz** (Swiss Transport Museum; www.verkehrshaus.ch; daily Apr–Oct 10am–6pm, Nov–Mar 10am–5pm), which is always being embellished and updated to keep up with technological progress, is the largest and most complete of its kind in Europe. The aeronautical section has dozens of early aeroplanes, as well as a reconstruction of the Zurich airport control tower, space capsules from the first American space flights and even a moon rock. In the huge section devoted to railway transport, you can find more than 60 real locomotives and a very faithful reproduction of a section of the Saint-Gotthard rail line. Swissorama, projected on to a circular screen, shows a 20-minute film on Switzerland, its culture, traditions and economy. The history of the automobile also has its place here, as do tourism, the postal and telecommunications industries and navigation by river, lake and sea – for, land-locked as it may be, Switzerland is nonetheless a nautical nation. Finally, the museum has a planetarium and an imax cinema.

The **Richard Wagner Museum** (www. richard-wagner-museum.ch; mid-Mar–Nov Tue–Sun 10am–noon, 2–5pm) occupies Haus Tribschen, the spacious home where the composer lived from 1866 to 1872. It was in this house that he married Cosima, Franz Lizst's daughter. The villa, built on a promontory and commanding a wonderful view, was so dear to Wagner that he declared, 'Nothing will make me leave this place.' (Later, of course, he left it for Bayreuth). The first floor has a selection of original scores, letters and photographs, along with Wagner's grand piano. Upstairs is the city's collection of antique and exotic instruments.

LAKE LUCERNE

The most delightful way to visit central Switzerland is to take a steamboat in summer – a motorboat in winter – and to drift down the **Vierwaldstättersee**  (Lake Lucerne).

The softly sloping banks of the Swiss plateau, with Mount Pilatus (2,129m/6,985ft; see page 73) in the background, give way little by little to the foothills of the lower Alps and their pastures, while the higher peaks tower majestically over the south end of the lake.

Löwendenkmal, the lion monument

Statue of William Tell in Altdorf

The bay of **Küssnacht** is best known for its many orchards and farms with pointed roofs. **Weggis**, **Vitznau** and **Beckenried** are pretty villages that invite you to wander or sit down for a meal. Across from Weggis, above the lake, **Bürgenstock**, once one of Europe's most famous ski resorts, still attracts a fashionable clientele. A fascinating one-hour walk brings you to the foot of the impressive Hammetschwand elevator, which gives access to a fabulous view.

The 28m (92ft) rock that rises from the water on the other side of the lake from **Brunnen** is called the Schillerstein. This 'pebble' is dedicated to the great German dramatist, Friedrich Schiller, who immortalised William Tell (see page 16) in a famous play. Oddly enough, Schiller never set foot in Switzerland.

A bit further along, the meadow of **Rütli** is the symbol of Swiss national unity: the birthplace of the Confederation, founded here in 1291 (see page 17), it was also the place chosen by General Henri Guisan, in 1940, to gather his top officers to organise a national defence strategy.

Lake Uri with its steep, fjord-like banks, is the wildest branch of the Vierwaldstättersee. While this entire region is particularly well suited to hiking, the 'Swiss Way' along the banks of Lake Uri is nothing less than a historical adventure for those who love to walk. Most places here are also accessible by other means (train, boat or bus). The **Tellskapelle**

(Chapel of Tell), on the east bank, is built on the very spot where William Tell is said to have leapt from the boat taking him to prison, thus escaping his jailers.

Flüelen, at the far end of the lake, was once the unloading dock for boats carrying merchandise destined for trade in Italy. The bundles were then loaded on to mules for the journey through the Gotthard pass. **Altdorf**, the county seat of the canton of Uri, owes its fame to William Tell, who shot the apple off his son's head here; at the Tellspielhaus, Schiller's play continually re-enacts the same victory.

THREE MOUNTAINS

Mount Pilatus . Considered the emblem of Lucerne, it was scaled for the first time in the 16th century. This was a courageous undertaking, not only because it required good mountaineering skills, but because the villagers, believing

Vierwaldstätersee (Lake Lucerne) viewed from a steamboat

the mountain to be haunted by the demonic spirit of Pontius Pilate (hence the name), forbade anyone access to it with threat of imprisonment.

Generally, visitors take the boat or the train to Alpnachstad, then the cog-wheel railway (the steepest route in the world, with a 48° grade; it runs only in summer), which leaves you with a five-minute walk to the top (2,132m/6,995ft), where the view is extensive. As an alternative route down, take the cable car from Kriens (www.pilatus.ch).

Mount Rigi. In good weather, there is a superb view from Rigi-Kuhn (1,800m/5,906ft) of the highest peaks of the Alps from Bern to Valais. This 'island in the sun' is accessible by

Mount Pilatus

cog train (from Vitznau or Goldau) or cable car (from Weggis). For timetables and fares, see www.rigi.ch.

Mount Titlis. Nearly twice as high as Rigi, it reaches 3,240m (10,630ft). First, go to **Engelberg**, a sunny ski resort whose Benedictine monastery was founded in the 17th century. Be sure to admire the abbey's baroque church; the organ here is the largest in the country. From the station, take the funicular, then the spectacular revolving cable car (www.titlis.ch), to arrive at Klein (Little) Titlis, where the snow never melts; here, you can explore an ice cave and marvel at the peaks of Oberland and the Valais Alps. It takes another hour on foot to cover the last 220m (720ft) of uneven terrain to the very top of Mount Titlis.

EAST OF LUCERNE

Whether they like it or not, statistics reveal that the citizens of Zug are the richest inhabitants of Switzerland. In international economy and finance circles, Zug is known as a fiscal paradise, which

The world's first revolving cable car, on Mount Titlis

explains the presence here of so many business firms and sumptuous villas.

Small, cosmopolitan and opulent, the town of **Zug** *(Zoug)* owes its charm to its ancient and perfectly preserved stone walls. Modern buildings blend with historic ones in a harmonious and original way. The Fischmarkt (fish market), the Untergasse and the Obergasse all evoke the Middle Ages. At the corner of the Fischmarkt and the Untergasse, the **Rathaus** (town hall) is remarkable for its magnificent Council Room. Among the vestiges of medieval fortifications, notice in particular the **Zytturm** (clock tower) on the Kolinplatz (ask for the key at the police station next door). Just steps away, the 15th- and 16th-century **Sankt-Oswalds-Kirche** (Saint Oswald's Church) deserves to be seen for the delicate sculptures above its main door. Be sure to continue your visit just behind this church to the exquisite **Burg**, which houses an historical museum.

For a town that gave its name to the whole country, **Schwyz** ⓰ is rather placid and much smaller than you might imagine. The **Bundesbriefmuseum** (www.bundesbrief.ch; Tue–Sun 10am–5pm) contains precious documents from the earliest days of the Confederation: the Pact of 1291, initialled by the representatives of the 13 original cantons (see page 17), and a series of charters, each marking a stage in the fascinating construction of the country.

Einsiedeln ⓱, one hour from Lucerne or Zurich, is an important pilgrimage site. Gigantic and imposing, its **Benedictine abbey** attracts many tourists. The history of Einsiedeln began more than 1,100 years ago when a monk, Meinrad, was murdered in his hermitage in the middle of the forest. A century later, he had become the object of cult worship, and some monks founded a monastery in his memory on the same site. The church and its surrounding 11th-century baroque buildings are considered the crowning achievement of their architect, Caspar Moosbrugger, a converted monk who lived in Einsiedeln for more than 40 years. At the centre of the complex is the abbey church, flanked by two towers. With its four courtyards, the complex rivals the Escorial in Spain for size. The gold-and-white interior is by the Asam brothers of Munich; Cosmas Damian painted the frescoes and Egid Quirin executed the stucco-work.

In the chapel built on the spot where Meinrad was killed is a small Black Madonna; pilgrims come here in the hope that she will grant their prayers. Gregorian chants sung by the monks, along with frequent organ concerts, make this an unforgettable visit. The **Fürstensaal** (Hall of Princes) is richly appointed, a reminder that before the 15th century the abbots of Einsiedeln were princes of the German empire.

Today, Einsiedeln is a self-sufficient community of around 100 monks and 50 lay brothers; they work at various trades ranging from mechanic to stonemason to baker. The monastery also operates a printing works, a stud farm and a cattle farm.

GRISONS

This canton holds three records: it is the biggest, the least populous, and the most polyglot in all Switzerland. It is, in fact, the only canton where three languages are spoken: German (60 percent), Romansh (22 percent) and Italian (13 percent). **Grisons** (Graubünden, Grischuns, Grigioni) occupies about one-sixth of the area

Benedictine abbey, Einsiedeln

of the country. This canton's most precious resource is the rough natural beauty it offers to visitors. Its history is closely linked to that of its 10 mountain passes. Even today, several of them remain major arteries of European communication.

The first settlers to leave their mark here were the Rhaetians, whose descendants still speak the Romansh language. In AD15, the Romans, seeking control over the mountain passes, conquered the Rhaetians. Later, the German emperors took it over for the same reason, imposing a feudal system on the area for centuries. In the 15th century, the peasants organised themselves in associations such as the Grey League (Grauer Bund), which gave its name to the Grisons mountain range. They threw off the yoke of the foreign princes and the Church. External pressure united these solid mountain folk, but they

Return of the bears

In 2005, Switzerland had its first reported bear sighting in more than 100 years in Grisons. Authorities have been trying to coax brown bears back into Swiss territory from Italy, but they had been unsuccessful until recently. Bears had been hunted to extinction in Switzerland more than a century ago.

could not remain independent forever. In 1803, after Napoleon's Act of Mediation, they joined the Confederation.

CHUR

The gateway to the region, **Chur** (Coire) is also the cantonal capital and main crossroads. Westward, you can climb, by way of Disentis, to the source of the Rhine; to the south, through the Julier or Albula passes, you can reach St Moritz and other famous ski resorts of Engadine; and to the east lie Davos and Klosters. To get from one valley to the next, you can choose between travelling by car, postal bus and the Rhätische Bahn, the regional narrow-gauge railway.

Chur is an active large town. You will love visiting its ancient winding streets and its oddly shaped town squares. To guide you in your wanderings, the local tourist office has organised two walks, marked in an original fashion: just follow the red or green footprints painted on the ground. Both routes leave from the Postplatz and take, respectively, 60 and 75 minutes. In the Poststrasse, the medieval **Rathaus** (town hall) has a lovely courtyard and several beautiful rooms.

The stone steps up the hill past the medieval gates lead to the **Bischöfliches Schloss** (Bishop's Palace), which has been the seat of the bishopric since the Middle Ages. Ahead of you looms the half-Romanesque, half-Gothic **cathedral**, majestic despite its irregular layout (the choir is too high and its axis is misaligned with that of the nave). An immense triptych in gilded woodwork crowns the altar. The treasury, one of the richest in Switzerland, contains many venerable reliquaries.

A fine 17th-century building houses the historical and folk-lore collections of the **Rhätisches Museum** (Rhetic Museum). The **Kunstmuseum** (Fine Arts Museum; www.buendner-kunstmuseum.ch; Tue–Sun 10am–5pm, Thu 10am–8pm), on the Postplatz, displays works from the 18th to the 20th century by Grison's artists (Giovanni, Augusto and Alberto Giacometti, and Angelika Kauffman, who emigrated to England).

Maienfeld (15 minutes by train from Chur, 20 by car) is a lovely village with some attractive bourgeois homes. An excellent red wine is made here, dry and light, and there is no shortage of inns in which to taste it. This is also the land of Heidi, the heroine of the popular children's book by Johanna Spyri.

The view looking down from the Bischöliches Schloss

After visiting Chur, you will find yourself within easy reach of several famous Grisons resorts.

Lenzerheide-Valbella, at 1,500m (4,921ft), draws visitors all year round. **Arosa** (1,740m/5,709 ft) is a charming spot surrounded by forested mountains reflected in two small lakes. Sports enthusiasts and romantics will both find what they want in this resort.

As for **Davos** ⓲ (1,560m/5,118ft), its international renown has grown since it began hosting the annual World Economic Forum.

Kids dressed as Heidi and Peter in Maienfeld

But its worldwide pull is not only recent. Thomas Mann made it the setting for his 1924 novel *The Magic Mountain*. Numerous sports facilities and a huge skiing area, shared with **Klosters** (1,180m/3,871ft), make this a popular year-round destination.

THE VORDERRHEIN

A picturesque route follows the course of the Vorderrhein (Upper Rhine) to its source, near Oberalp pass, on the way to Andermatt and Saint-Gotthard. At **Reichenau**, you enter into the lush green Vorderrhein valley, where the Upper and Lower Rhine unite to form the single great river that flows through Germany and Holland to the North Sea.

Past this small town, the valley narrows and the route rises to the sunny ski town of **Flims** (1,080m/3,545ft), made up of two parts, Flims-Dorf and Flims-Waldhaus; the latter is where you will find the hotels, scattered through a dense forest of pines and larch, interspersed with sparkling lakes. Below Flims is **Laax**, a much smaller town with an interesting baroque church that dates from the end of the 17th century. **Ilanz** proudly calls itself the first city on the Rhine, basing its claims on 1,200 years of history. In **Trun**, visit the impressive 17th-century residence of the abbots of Disentis (now a museum of local art and folklore).

In **Disentis** ⑲, the great 12th-century abbey testifies to the importance of this town as a religious centre in the Middle Ages. The current monastery dates from the 17th century, while the baroque abbey church *(Klosterkirche)* was built over the tomb of Sigisbert, the hermit-monk, in the 18th century.

THE HINTERRHEIN

To reach Ticino, you can go through the Hinterrheintal, or valley of the lower Rhine, in the direction of the San Bernardino pass. After the **Domleschg valley**, with its villages and castles, you pass Thusis to reach the **Via Mala**: harsh and arid, this canyon carved out by the frothing Rhine is now perfectly accessible. The 'bad way' *(via mala)* opens out into the Schams (or Schons) valley. The jewel of this region is **Zillis** ⓴, where a 12th-century church harbours the oldest **painted ceiling** in Europe. The 153 panels of St Martin's church were inspired by the New Testament and the lives of Christ and St Martin.

Looking over the Rhine Gorge, Flims Region

After the endearing village of Andeer, you enter the Rheinwald. **Splügen**, a town favoured by hikers, is also a crossroads: on one side, the Splügen pass leads to Italy; on the other, the San Bernardino pass is the gateway to Ticino.

ENGADINE

In the valley of the River Inn (or En), which gives **Engadine** its name, the contrast between the ancient villages and the ultramodern resorts is striking. The former are made up of sturdy stone houses with their unique and beautiful *sgraffiti* decorations. This technique consists in covering a dark stucco wall with a white coating, into which a pattern is then scratched in places to reveal the darker layer beneath.

12th-century ceiling, Zilis

Engadine is divided into two regions, lower and upper, both served by trains from Chur. The first stretches from Maloja to Zernez. From Chur Postbuses cross the Julier or Albula passes. Lower Engadine extends from Zernez to Martina, on the Austrian border; from Davos or Klosters, you can get here through the Flüela pass.

The village of **Guarda**, in lower Engadine, has preserved its tiny paved streets, its fountains, and its intricately worked houses. If you are curious about local architecture and folklore, be sure to make a stop here. Another very pretty village is **Scuol** (*Schuls* in German), the eastern terminus of the Rhätische Bahn. This dynamic little town, like its neighbours Tarasp and Vulpera, has its own thermal baths.

On the border between lower and upper Engadine, **Zernez** is the main gateway to the **Swiss National Park ㉑**. Begin with a visit to the Park House, where you can get all the information you need and also watch an audiovisual presentation on the park. The park itself is small (160 sq km/100 sq miles) and very well preserved: you could forget about the human race here, if not for the signs indicating (very clearly) the paths for forest walks. The best time to visit is from mid-June to the end of October, when the Park House is open. The flora is particularly varied because of the very hilly terrain, and you may catch a glimpse of such unusual animals as ibex, elk, marmots and vultures.

The Ofen pass (Fuorn pass/Pass dal Fuorn), just past the park, takes you to **Müstair** ('monastery' in Romansh), the main village of the wooded valley of the same name, situated at the Italian border. During the Reformation, the towns of the region converted to Protestantism, but Müstair, barricaded behind the walls of its monastery, remained Catholic. Here, Romansh is king.

At the end of the village, the **Abbey of St John the Baptist** was founded in the 8th century by a Bishop of Chur who was related to Charlemagne. (Tradition has it that Charlemagne himself was responsible for its foundation.) The church, with its triple apse, underwent transformations in the 15th century. The wall paintings are some of the finest remaining examples of the Carolingian period (the first half of the 9th century). Also, note the 12th-century statue of Charlemagne.

Back in the Inn valley, stop at **Zuoz**, a quaint, well-preserved town. It has a church with windows by Giacometti and a group of typical Engadine houses around the main square that date from the 16th to 18th centuries.

St Moritz ㉒, a world-renowned ski resort, attracts a rich and cosmopolitan clientele. The success of St Moritz – the birthplace of Alpine winter sports in 1884 – is justified by its favoured natural setting, dry and sunny climate, elaborate recreational facilities and a carefully maintained reputation for elegance. This region, a paradise of snow sports, offers infinite possibilities. Its bobsled and skeleton slopes are very famous (see page 132). The village is roughly divided into two parts: St Moritz-Bad, where the thermal baths are located, and, on the hill, St Moritz-Dorf, with its palatial hotels.

Worthy of note are two museums: the **Engadine Museum** (furniture, tile stoves and historic weapons through the ages; www.engadiner-museum.ch) and the **Segantini Museum** (www.segantini-museum.ch), which has landscapes by the Italian painter Giovanni Segantini inspired by views of the Engadine region.

Northeast of St Moritz, ride the funicular to **Muottas Muragl**, a panoramic vista point from which you can survey all of the

GLACIER EXPRESS

There's no excuse for missing the Glacier Express (www.glacier express.ch) that links St Moritz to Zermatt. This 71/2-hour railway trip across the Alps, with a summit at the Oberalp pass, is spell-binding. Panoramic windows in each carriage offer an exciting spectacle both in winter and in summer. The train goes through 91 tunnels, crosses 291 bridges and takes hairpin turns that will leave you with goosebumps.

Skier on the slopes of St Moritz

upper Engadine. See if you can spot Pontresina, the lakes of St Moritz and Silvaplana, and Sils (where Nietzsche stayed while writing *Thus Spoke Zarathustra*). Even further out is the Maloja pass. Or climb higher to the Piz Nair (3,057m/10,030ft), reachable by funicular, then cable car, and finally by foot (15 minutes).

Pontresina (1,803m/5,915ft), on the Bernina Pass road, has some beautiful ski slopes. A base for alpinists – you will find the largest climbing school in Switzerland here – it offers hiking trails as well. The glacier trail at Morteratsch has signs explaining the formation of moraines, deposits of earth and stone left by moving glaciers.

Whether you go through the Bernina Pass in a car, train or bus, you will never forget the sights afforded by this route into the Poschiavo Valley: the Morteratsch glacier, the **Diavolezza** panorama, the Piz Palü and, on the other side of the pass, the Alpine garden of Alp Grüm. In this valley, Italian is spoken; in fact, all over Poschiavo, you can sense the Mediterranean atmosphere.

Taking a refreshing break in Morcote, Ticino

TICINO

When you arrive in **Ticino** from Grisons, you suddenly find yourself in the thick of Italian conversation, music and food, basking in a sunny and charming atmosphere that seems to have been lifted straight out of neighbouring Italy. Tourists are drawn here by the picturesque villages and lakes, the deep valleys that take you back to another age, the many cultural offerings, and a dazzling array of outdoor activities, including walking, sailing and skiing.

Ticino is closer to Milan than it is to Bern, and its ties to Italy, especially the cultural ones, are very strong. Ticino was torn from the Milanese by the Swiss in the 15th century and dominated by the cantons on the other side of the Saint Gotthard pass until 1803, when it was made a canton of its own. This attachment to the Confederation is all the more remarkable given that, until the end of the 19th century – that is, until the construction of the Gotthard railway tunnel – the canton spent every winter cut off from the rest of Switzerland. The road tunnel was not finished until 1980.

BELLINZONA

The capital of Ticino, **Bellinzona** ㉓ guards the way to three mountain passes – Saint Gotthard, Lukmanier and San Bernardino – which explains the town's turbulent history. It was a coveted location, fought over by the Romans, the

Franks, the Lombards and the Swiss of the Confederation. Beautiful Lombard-style arches, pastel-coloured houses with balconies, and old churches make up the heart of Bellinzona. Not to be missed are the three medieval castles surrounded by **crenellated walls**.

The **Castelgrande** (Nov–Mar 11am–4pm, Apr–June, Sep–Oct 10am–6pm, July–Aug 10am–7pm Mon 10am–6pm, Tue–Sun 9am–10pm; combination ticket for all three castles available) or Castel Vecchio, dating originally from the 4th century ad, has been creatively restored by the architect Aurelio Galfetti. This group of buildings includes a historical museum, theatres and two restaurants. The second, the **Castello di Montebello** (daily Apr–June, Sep–Nov 10am–6pm, July–Aug 10am–7pm), was built from the 13th to the 15th century. It was restored in 1903 (exterior) and during the 1970s (interior). A museum of archaeology and history,

Picturesque mountains in Ticino

A crowd watches performers outside Castello di Montebello

the Museo Civico, has been installed here: it displays pieces found in archaeological digs all over the canton. The third castle, which towers above the two others, is the 15th-century **Castello di Sasso Corbaro** (Apr–June, Sep–Nov 10am–6pm, July–Aug 10am–7pm). It was built in some six months of day and night labour by order of the Duke of Milan, who feared an imminent offensive by the Swiss. Bellinzona's three fortresses are often called by their nicknames – Uri, Schwyz and Unterwald – in memory of the baillifs sent by the Waldstätten in the 16th century to rule over the region.

LOCARNO AND LAKE MAGGIORE

West of Bellinzona, on Lake Maggiore, **Locarno** 24 luxuriates in a warm and sunny climate, with orange trees, banana plants and palm trees growing in abundance year-round.

The best-known monument in Locarno is the **Madonna del Sasso**, five minutes from the centre of town by funicular. For centuries, pilgrims have climbed the steep path to its sanctuary. The church, which is perched on a rocky cliff, seems immense from a distance, but this impression lessens upon entering, perhaps because of the huge number of artworks that are housed inside it.

From here hikers and, in winter, skiers can take the cable car up the steep flanks of Mount Cardada, a trip of just a few minutes. A ski lift takes you the rest of the way to the **Cimetta** (1,671m/5,482ft), a superb belvedere, where the view of lake and town is truly breathtaking.

Once back 'on land', those who love art and history should make a point of visiting the **Castello Visconti**, which was partially restored in the 1920s. The arch-lined 15th-century courtyard bears witness to the lost splendour of the castle's fortifications. Within the castle is the Museo Civico, a rich archaeological collection with many relics that date as far back as the Roman Empire (Tue–Sun 10am–noon, 2–5pm).

Follow the Via Rusca to the **Piazza Grande**, the main square of Locarno, lined with shops and cafés, which hosts the screenings and ceremonies of the **International Film Festival** each August (www.pardo.ch).

MODERN ARCHITECTURE

Lugano, like Bellinzona, Locarno, and other cities in Ticino, has many excellent examples of modern architecture. In fact, since the end of the 1960s, Ticino has seen the development of several generations of talented architects, whose international renown has inspired local authorities to invest in sizeable architectural undertakings. (A detailed and interesting history of this phenomenon, entitled *Discovering Modern Architecture in the Ticino*, is available from tourist offices throughout the canton.)

Examples include a series of creations by Mario Botta: the Banca del Gottardo (1988, viale Stefano Franscini), the Palazzo Telecom (1997 in Bellinzona) and the Palazzo Botta (1991, via Ciani 16, Lugano). Also of note are the Architect's Studio (1994 in Mendrisio) by Ivano Gianola and the Palazzo delle Pose (1996 in Locarno) by Livio Vacchini.

Up the hill, the **Città Vecchia** (Old Town) has an appealing combination of stately villas, time-worn tenements, hidden gardens and venerable churches. The Casa Rusca, on the Piazza Sant Antonio, contains works from the collection of Jean Arp (who died in Locarno in 1966), a leading Surrealist and one of the founders of the Dadaist art movement, as well as other donations.

Lake Maggiore 25 *(Lago Maggiore)*, shared by Italy and Switzerland, is popular with excursionists and lovers of water sports. The **Isles of Brissago** make a fun day trip. On San Pancrazio, the largest, is the **Botanical Garden**, devoted to exotic plants – bamboo, sugar cane, cactus – and all manner of citrus trees. Some boats continue toward Stresa to the Borromeo Islands, in Italian waters.

Ascona 26 is separated from Locarno only by the mouth of the River Maggia. Once a simple fishing village, this fashionable little town has long played host to artists and intellectuals: Isadora Duncan, Paul Klee and Lenin all stayed here. Also contributing to its fame are the frequent art exhibitions that are hosted here and an annual jazz festival (www.jazzascona.ch).

From Locarno or Ascona, a day trip is enough to explore the surrounding high, isolated valleys. If you're in good shape, you can explore the valleys on foot (maps of walking trails are available in tourist offices); alternatively, you can travel by car or postal bus. The wild and magnificent **Val Verzasca**, will not fail to move you. The most remote village, **Sonogno**, is only 31km (19 miles) from Locarno, but the contrast between it and the luxurious prosperity of the lakeside could not be more striking. The simple houses of Sonogno are entirely constructed of dry stones balanced one on another without any mortar.

The **Valle Maggia** follows the meandering River Maggia, northeast of Ascona and Locarno. Italianate architecture in all its variations is universal here – until you reach the wooden

chalets of the remote village of **Bosco** *(Gurin)*, in a side valley settled in the 12th century by emigrants from the canton
of Valais. Their descendants still speak an obscure Swiss-
German dialect that is unique in Ticino.

The **Centovalli**, which links Locarno with Domodossola, is
delightfully twisty, while the Onsernone valley is rough but
authentic nonetheless.

LUGANO AND ITS LAKE

First town of Ticino, **Lugano** ㉗ sweeps gently down between
two mountains and slopes to a shaded lakefront promenade.
Yachts and tourist boats ply the lake, while pleasant villages
cling to jagged outcroppings along its shore.

Here, the sun shines for more than 2,000 hours each year.
Forsythias and mimosas blossom in February; March is the
time for camellias, magnolias and peach trees; while April

The wild and wonderful Val Verzasca

glows with azaleas, rhododendrons, wisteria and Japanese cherry trees in bloom. The main square, **Piazza della Riforma**, is a vast space devoted to row upon row of café tables; you can linger here indefinitely, sipping an espresso or an aperitif. Covered shopping streets filled with boutiques lead from the plaza into the old town.

Facing the lake at the southern end of the Via Nassa is the tiny church of **Santa Maria degli Angioli** (St Mary of the Angels), with the finest Renaissance frescoes in Ticino. The most famous cycle, painted at the beginning of the 16th century, is a luminous *Passion of Christ* by Bernardino Luini, a student of Leonardo da Vinci; the same artist also decorated one of the side chapels.

Along the lake, the beautifully landscaped Parco Civico can provide a quiet respite with a display of flowers that are often changed to reflect the different seasons. Art lovers can visit the **Fine Arts Museum** in Villa Ciani in the park for occasional

Alfresco dining in the Piazza della Riforma

temporary exhibitions (Tue–Sun 10am–6pm). The Museo d'arte della Svizzera italiana (www.museo-cantonale-arte.ch; Tue 2–5pm, Wed–Sun 10am–5pm), previously known as the **Cantonal Art Museum**, occupies three buildings built between the 15th and 19th centuries at Via Canova 10 and hosts a permanent collection. The main building (www.masilugano.ch; Tue–Wed, Sun 10.30am–6pm, Thu–Sat 10.30am–8pm) focuses on 20th-century contemporary art, and features a number of temporary exhibitions.

An enthusiastic journalist once called Lugano 'the Rio of Europe'. For him, Mount San Salvatore was nothing less than a little brother of the Sugarloaf. To see if he was right, take a look – the best view is from **Mount Brè** 🕸 (accessible by funicular; www.montebre.ch). San Salvatore itself (912m/2,992ft) can be reached by funicular as well, for fabulous views and pleasant hiking trails back to the town.

A cruise on the lake will allow you to marvel at the peaks surrounding it and to see, or stop and visit, some quaint villages.

Gandria. Many artists have been attracted to this fishing village covered in flowers, yet Gandria, located northeast of Lugano, has never lost its authenticity.

Melide, south of Lugano, can be reached by land or water. Since 1959, millions have come to this village to lose themselves in the labyrinthine world of **Swissminiatur** 🕸 (www. swissminiatur.ch; daily mid-Mar–Oct 9am–6pm, July Sun–Thu 9am–8pm, Fri–Sat 9am–10pm), a model built to 1:25 scale of more than 100 national monuments. Trains glide on their tracks through tunnels and mountains, funiculars scale the peaks and boats drift by... the exhibition is fascinating and complete down to the last detail.

Morcote is an adorable village nestled into a hill. A long stone staircase from the 17th century takes you up a steep slope to the medieval chapel of Saint-Antoine. Further up, a

Trekking in Valais

slender belltower marks the **church of Santa Maria del Sasso** and its cemetery, full of towering cypress trees.

VALAIS

Since prehistoric times, the long, wide, untamed valley that bears the name of **Valais** (*Wallis* in German) has been an important means of communication between northern and southern as well as eastern and western Europe. In fact, Valais is really a continuation of the Rhône Valley; that great river, beginning as a melted glacier, finally empties its waters into Lake Geneva.

Here nature defies the imagination: waterfalls drop down the sheerest of cliffs while glaciers blind you with their whiteness. There are orchards in full bloom, rugged vineyards, mythical summits and cowbells tinkling in the mountain pastures. The mountains to the north protect the valley against cold winds and often rain, while the orientation of the side valleys to the *Föhn* (a characteristic warm, dry wind) gives the region a gentle climate.

Each of the adjacent valleys has its own customs and traditions. Halfway into Valais, somewhere around Sierre, the French language gives way to Swiss-German. But the linguistic division and cultural diversity of this canton doesn't seem to prevent the cohesion of its inhabitants, who are united by a strong Catholic faith.

After its domination by the Romans, Valais was controlled by the Burgundians. During the 15th century, the King of Burgundy bequeathed it to the bishops of Sion, whose influence made it impermeable to the Protestant Reformation. But there was no resisting the occupation by France after the Revolution in 1798. Made its own independent state by Bonaparte, Valais became a French *département* – known as Simplon – before finally joining the Confederation in 1815.

We will survey the length of this valley, rich in churches and monasteries, from Saint-Maurice to the sources of the Rhône, losing ourselves from time to time in the valleys along the side.

LOWER VALAIS

Above Monthey, **Champéry** (1,050m/3,445ft) offers lovers of winter sports access to a huge ski domain, **Portes du Soleil**,

ST BERNARDS

The famous St Bernard dogs are synonymous with Switzerland and her mountains. At a hospice, located at the Grand St Bernard Pass, these iconic dogs have been bred since the 18th century. A line of monks beginning with Bernard of Menthon have inhabited the hospice since the 11th century and still live on the site (guests can stay there, but the accommodation is modest). This idyllic location, right on the Italian-Swiss border, has a museum about the pass and the famous dogs, plus a kennel. The monks recently sold the kennel to a private foundation, but the dogs can still be visited here during the summer months when the pass is open (approximately June–early October). In winter, the dogs can be visited at a new kennel in the town of Martigny, not far from the pass. Every year a limited number of St Bernard puppies can be bought for around 2,000 Swiss Francs each. Call 027 722 6542 for visiting times or visit www.fondation-barry.ch for further information.

A lake in Valais with the snowcapped Weisshorn behind

which reaches all the way to France. In summer, more than 200km (125 miles) of groomed slopes await the eager mountain biker.

Back in the main valley, stop at the town of **Saint Maurice 30**, wedged between a precipitous cliff and a mountain range. The **Abbaye de Saint-Maurice** is among the oldest monastic institutions in Christendom. For nearly 14 centuries monks, and later canons, have been singing their psalms here. All this fervour commemorates Maurice, a Christian officer of the Roman Army who, because he had refused to worship the Roman gods, was massacred with his followers, some 6,000 men, around the year 285.

Since the 4th century, pilgrims (among them princes of Christendom) have come to place their offerings on the martyrs' tombs. These accumulated gifts make up the **treasury**, which includes some exceptional pieces of silversmith work.

Martigny 31, located at a sharp angle along the Rhône riverbank, has long been an important crossroads. Its old town contains the ruins of a Roman amphitheatre, which could hold 6,000 spectators. On a fortification to the west stands the Bâtiaz, the stark tower (now restored) of a 13th-century castle. Finally, outside the centre of town, an audacious architectural complex is home to the **Pierre-Gianadda Foundation** (www.gianadda.ch; daily June–Nov 9am–7pm, Nov–June 10am–6pm), which brings together a museum of Roman antiquities, an automobile museum and a cultural centre that organises high-quality temporary exhibitions in partnership with other galleries abroad as well as concerts and plays. The park is full of statues by Rodin, Brancusi, Miró, Moore, Dubuffet and others.

If you are hurrying to get across the Alps you can take the train or drive along the E27 with its almost 6-km (4-mile) long tunnel that connects Switzerland and Italy. By doing this you will avoid the difficult road that runs across the **Grand St Bernard Pass** (2,740m/8,100ft high) and which is closed all winter. But it also means you'll miss the famous **hospice** founded by Saint Bernard of Menthon. There is a museum here which is full of artifacts from Napoleon's passage through the pass, with 40,000 men on their way to the battle of Marengo in 1800. In the kennel, friendly St Bernard dogs are raised and trained to rescue avalanche victims (see page 95).

SION AND ENVIRONS

Nearly 1,000 years ago, when bishop-princes held sovereign authority over the whole of Valais, **Sion** added a politico-religious role to its traditional military one. The most famous of its bishops, Cardinal Matthew Schiner (1465–1522), is still the hero of the canton, even though his

Eroding rock formations near the village of Euseigne

Swiss pyramids

The Val d'Herens, southeast of Sion, contains a relic from the Ice Age: the so-called Pyramides d'Euseigne, earth pillars protected from erosion by the flat stones which cap them.

schemes – he pushed the then-young Confederation to ally itself with the Pope, sending it into war with the King of France – finally led to the defeat of the Swiss at Marignano.

Sion, the capital of Valais, is overlooked by two imposing hills. The first, Tourbillon, the hill closest to the mountains, is crowned by the ruins of a 13th-century episcopal castle. The second, Valère, closer to the river and the centre of town, supports an imposing fortified church (June–Sept daily 10am–6pm, Oct–May Tue–Sun 10am–5pm). This Romanesque-Gothic structure, once the cathedral of Sion, is known for its naïve stone carving, 15th-century frescoes, and choir stalls from the 17th century. The organ, constructed at the beginning of the 10th century, is one of the oldest functioning organs in Europe.

Between the hills, in Rue des Châteaux, there are two more museums of interest: the **Art Museum** in Place de la Majorie (open Oct–May Tues–Sun 11am–5pm, June–Sept Tue–Sun 11am–6pm), once the residence of church officials, now holds the Musée Cantonal des Beaux-Arts (Cantonal Fine Arts Museum); and the modern **Espace d'archéologie de la Grange-à-l'Evêque** (June–Sept Tue–Sun 11am–6pm, Oct–May Tue–Sun 11am–5pm), on the other side of the street, which brings together objects found at archaeological digs all over the canton.

In the heart of town, you will see the 17th-century town hall, painted pink; the astronomical belfry clock is from 1667. The **cathedral** (Notre-Dame-du-Glarier), in late Gothic style, was built after a fire destroyed the original Romanesque edifice, whose belltower is all that remains.

Sion is a good starting point for day trips to the neighbouring ski resorts. To the north, **Crans-Montana** 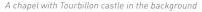 offers exceptional ski slopes; it also has facilities for tennis and golf, and various places to shop. Food-lovers will not be disappointed with the cuisine, and night-crawlers may run into holidaying celebrities.

To the south, the **Val d'Herens** is known for its picturesque villages with dark wood chalets, generously hung with red geraniums in summer. **Evolène** is an authentic old village, and **Arolla** (2,000m/6,562ft), to the south, is a centre for mountain climbing.

At the bottom of the Hérémence valley, the 285-m (935-ft) tall **Grande Dixence dam** offers was the tallest dam in the world until 1980. You can arrange to visit from mid-June to September (tel: 027 328 43 11; www.grande-dixence.ch).

Continuing down the Rhône to the east, you will reach the last bastion of the French language, announced by

A chapel with Tourbillon castle in the background

Leukerbad's baths

With six public baths and a number of hotels offering their own thermal bathing options, Leukerbad (www.leukerbad.ch) is an ideal location for relaxation. The temperature at the source is 51°C (124°F), and about 3.9 million litres (860,000 gallons) of natural hot water flows daily into the private and public baths, giving this area the largest amount of thermal water in all of Europe.

a sign in two languages: **Sierre/Siders**. Surrounded by vineyards, the town enjoys a particularly dry climate. Taste vintage wines in any one of a number of cellars, or learn about viticultural techniques in the **Valaisian Museum of Wines and Winemaking** (www.museeduvin-valais.ch; Mar–Nov Tues–Fri 2–6pm, Sat–Sun 11am–6pm).

On a detour to the south of Sierre, nestled in the **Val d'Anniviers**, you will find **Chandolin** (1,935m/6,345ft), one of the highest European villages that is inhabited year round, as well as a few other charming mountain resorts, including St-Luc, Grimentz and Zinal, all of which are dwarfed by two mountains: Mount Weisshorn (4,505m/14,780ft) and the Zinalrothorn (4,220m/13,848ft).

Past Sierre, in the Rhône valley, **Leuk** (Loèche) can be recognised by its castles and towers dating from the era of the 'majors' (church officials of Sion). The hiking route through the Gemmi Pass, leading to Kandersteg (Bernese Oberland), leaves from **Leukerbad** (Loèche-les-Bains), an upland spa and centre for hiking and mountain climbing.

From Gampel, approximately halfway between Sierre and Brig, a road leads steeply to **Lötschental**, a high, wild valley which was unreachable in winter for centuries. That is, until 1913, when the 15-km (10-mile) long rail tunnel that links Valais to the Bernese Oberland was inaugurated. Pause in **Kippel** and stroll around the church. The

Lötschentaler Museum (www.loetschentalermuseum.ch) reveals the secrets of this mysterious valley.

UPPER VALAIS

The most famous mountain in Valais, the **Matterhorn** (*Mont Cervin/Monte Cervino*, 4,478m/14,692ft) is, if not the highest in the Alps, certainly the most impressive. This formidable horn-shaped peak has never ceased to be a challenge to mountaineers the world over.

The first expedition to reach the top was led by a young Englishman, Edward Whymper. His team scaled the north-eastern face of the mountain. But the conquest, on 14 July 1865, did little to dispel the terror that the Matterhorn has always inspired. On the contrary, it reinforced it: on their descent, four of Whymper's six companions fell to their deaths.

The **Alpine Museum in Zermatt** ❸❹ retraces the history of the conquest of the Matterhorn. This famous resort town has often served as a base for Alpine expeditions. From Visp (*Viège*) in the Rhône Valley, the train heads up the Mattertal (37km/23 miles) to arrive at the resort, where cars are prohibited and sleds, carriages and electric carts are the sole

The chateau de Villa in Sierre houses a wine museum

Swimming in an outdoor thermal pool in Valais

means of transport. (Cars have to stop at the village of Täsch. Trains run every 20 minutes during the day to Zermatt.) Zermatt offers comfortable lodgings and high-altitude skiing year round. A cog-wheel railway will take you to **Gornergrat** (3,135m/10,285ft; www.gornergrat.ch), with an unforgettable view of **Monte Rosa**, the highest mountain in Switzerland at 4,634m/15,203ft.

If you're not afraid of heights, take the four successive cable cars to the **Little Matterhorn**: the fourth, overlooking the glacier, deposits you at the highest ski resort in Europe (3,820m/12,533ft).

In a parallel valley nestles another famous resort, **Saas-Fee** ㉟, dominated by several mountains topping 4,000m (13,100ft). Cars are not permitted (you may park in a special area provided at the entrance). A subway links Fleskinn to Mittelallalin, 3,500m (11,483ft) up, where the **Ice Palace** awaits you. In a cave of more than 5,000 cu m (16,400cu ft), you can discover the secrets of 1,000-year-old glaciers.

Although the Swiss have mixed feelings towards Napoleon, **Brig** has nonetheless named one of its streets after the great man. He built the Simplon Pass road, which begins here, through the Alps. This town is dominated by the three onion-shaped domes of the **Stockalper Castle**, built by Kaspar Jodok von Stockalper (1609–91), a very wealthy businessman. The **Simplon Pass** (2,005m/6,578ft), only 25km (16 miles) away, is the high point of a spectacular road, all gorges and steep embankments, which winds its way into Italy.

Heading back north-east up the Rhône Valley is the summer and winter sports resort of Bettmeralp (www.aletsch arena.ch). This region serves as an excellent launching point to see the **Aletsch glacier** , the longest in Switzerland. At the furthest point of the Rhône Valley, which is called Goms Valley after the village of Oberwald, is the **Furka Pass**. At 2,430m (7,976ft), it is a vital link between the east and the west of Switzerland and offers an incomparable view on to the peaks of the Bernese Oberland. Just before the pass, you can stop for a close look at the **Rhône glacier** ㊲, an impressive example of a glacial retreat. The **ice cave** is open from June to October.

Zermatt, in the upper Matter Valley with the Matterhorn beyond

GENEVA

Geneva ❸ is Switzerland's second largest city after Zurich and capital of the tiny canton of the same name. It is far more cosmopolitan than any other Swiss city – not just because of its location right next to the French border but also because it is the base of numerous international organisations as well as European seat of the United Nations. The population is just as diverse; approximately 40 percent are foreigners.

Geneva's location at the western tip of Lake Geneva has been considered a strategic one since 58 BC, when Julius Caesar and his troops destroyed the ancient bridge over the Rhône to halt the movement of Helvetian troops toward Gaul. Since then, many a sovereign has coveted Geneva as a communications nexus and a centre of trade. Thus, the city has been under the control of the dukes of Burgundy, the German emperor, the dukes of Savoy and, briefly, Napoleon Bonaparte.

In 1602, several thousand mercenaries brought in by the Duke of Savoy besieged the city. Taking advantage of a particularly dark night, they scaled the city walls, but the spears wielded by Geneva's men, along with the boiling soup hurled by its women, got the better of them. Each year around 11 December, the *Escalade* (Scaling of the Walls) is commemorated by a torchlight procession and a series of masked balls.

The French theologian Jean Calvin made Geneva a great centre of Protestantism, and from 1541 Protestant refugees and pilgrims flowed into the 'Protestant Rome'. Today, tolerance reigns. The city is the seat of the ecumenical World Council of Churches and contains several Protestant, Catholic and Orthodox churches, a synagogue and a mosque.

In 1920, American president Woodrow Wilson made Geneva the world capital of diplomacy by choosing it to be the seat for the League of Nations. The city, which had so long been a centre for banking and watchmaking, was thrust onto the world stage, and since then numerous international agencies, including the International Committee of the Red Cross (ICRC), the World Health Organization (WHO), the World Trade Organisation (ETO) and the European Free Trade Association (EFTA) have chosen Geneva as their home.

A STROLL THROUGH THE CITY

The tallest monument in Geneva and a symbol of the city, the **Water Jet**  *(Jet d'Eau)* is visible from many parts of town: its jet of water reaches the height of a 40-storey building.

Relaxing in the sun with a view of the Water Jet

The imposing Mont-Blanc bridge links the two parts of town. Here, you will see the sudden narrowing at the spot where the lake becomes a powerful river: the Rhône, which enters the lake at one end and exits at the other. From the bridge on the right bank, Mont Blanc can often be seen peeking out from the French Alps to the south. To the west of the bridge is Rousseau Island, accessible on foot by the Bergues bridge. The statue facing the lake is of writer and philosopher Jean-Jacques Rousseau (1712–78). Downstream, the river is split in two by what the Genevans call simply the Island. Only a watchtower remains of the castle built here in 1219.

At the other side of the bridge you enter the luxurious **shopping district**. Wander down the rue du Rhône, the rue de la Confédération, the rue du Marché, the rue de la Croix-d'Or and the rue de la Corraterie – an elegant boulevard that ends at the place Neuve. Three impressive buildings are here: the **Grand Théâtre** (inspired by the Opéra Garnier in Paris), the **Conservatoire de Musique** and the **Musée Rath**, a sublime Greek-style structure constructed in 1826 as the first fine-arts museum in Switzerland.

Walking through the main shopping district

Place Neuve opens into the tree-lined promenade des Bastions. On the left is the **Reformation Monument**. Erected in 1909, the 400th anniversary of the birth of Calvin, this 100-m (330-ft) long wall bears religious inscriptions in several languages. The group of sculptures at the centre represents Calvin and the French reformers Théodore de Bèze and Guillaume Farel as well as the Scottish preacher John Knox. Facing the monument is the main building of the **University of Geneva**, which is the offspring of Calvin's Theological Academy.

THE OLD CITY

The Old City is a maze of streets and historic dwellings. If you take the rue Saint-Léger at the end of the promenade des Bastions, you will arrive at the **place du Bourg-de-Four**, with its attractive fountain, surrounded by the Palais de Justice (1712) and some lovely houses (16th–18th centuries). Occupying the highest point in the Old City is the **Cathédrale Saint-Pierre ❸**. This has been a place of worship of some kind since pagan antiquity. In the 12th century, its construction began first in the Romanesque and later in the Gothic style. In the 18th century, the façade was adorned with classical columns that still provoke controversy today. The interior is as austere as the doctrine Calvin preached here for more than 20 years. From the top of the northern tower (take the lift), there's an exceptional **view** of Geneva and surrounding areas.

Just around the corner from the cathedral is a new museum devoted to the Reformation, **Musée International de la Réforme** (www.musee-reforme.ch; Tue–Sun 10am–5pm). With films, rare books and manuscripts, the importance of Geneva is tied into the overall history of the Reformation.

The **Tavel House** (the Museum of Old Geneva; Tue–Sun 11am–6pm; free), on the rue du Puits-Saint-Pierre, is the oldest dwelling in Geneva. On the corner of the rue de l'Hôtel-de-Ville, be sure to notice the **Arsenal**, with a line-up of 17th- and 18th-century cannon under its arches. The three wall mosaics, dating from 1949, represent important episodes in the city's history. On the other side of the street, the **Hôtel de Ville ❻** (town hall), seat of the cantonal government, has an elegant Renaissance courtyard where concerts can be heard in summer. In this building, the Geneva Convention, the first convention agreement on the treatment of prisoners of war, was signed in 1864.

Just past the Hôtel de Ville, follow the picturesque **Grand-Rue**, lined with buildings from the 15th to the 18th century;

Rousseau's birthplace

one of them, No. 34, was once the workshop of the painter Ferdinand Hodler. A little further down, No. 40 is the birthplace of Rousseau. A small museum, **Espace Rousseau**, devoted to his life is located here (Tue–Sun 11am–5.30pm). Parallel to this street, the **rue des Granges**, a bastion of the great bourgeois families of Geneva, distinguishes itself by its beautiful Louis XVI-style houses.

INTERNATIONAL CITY

The vast **Palais des Nations** (www.unog.ch; tours Apr–Aug Mon–Sat 10am–noon, 2–4pm; Sep–Mar Mon–Fri 10am–noon, 2–4pm), conceived as the headquarters of the League of Nations, was inaugurated in 1937, with the spectre of war already looming over attempts at international cooperation. After World War II, the newly gathered United Nations claimed the building, at the heart of Ariana Park, as its European headquarters. Guided tours take you through the historic rooms, notably the Council Hall, which has remarkable frescoes, the enormous Assembly Hall, and a peek at one of the conference rooms.

For a moving look at the history of the Red Cross, visit the **Musée International de la Croix-Rouge et du Croissant-Rouge** (www.micr.org; Nov–Mar Tue–Sun 10am–5pm, Apr–Oct 10am–6pm), next door to the Palais des Nations, for an understanding of the important work of the organisation from its beginnings to the present day.

PARKS AND GARDENS

Geneva is rightly proud of its huge parks, with their fountains, sculptures, pavilions and cafés. The **English Garden** , on the left bank, is known mainly for its giant floral clock, 5m/16ft in diameter, whose immense face is made up of thousands of flowers and plants, replanted twice each year. The clock symbolises Geneva's watchmaking industry. By the water, you will also find boats that leave to many destinations along the lake, including some in France.

On the right bank, Geneva's most pompous monument, the mausoleum of the Duke of Brunswick (1804–73), presides over the **Jardin Brunswick** (Brunswick Garden) on quai du Mont-Blanc. The duke, who spent his last years in exile in Geneva, left his immense fortune to the city on the condition that a mausoleum be erected in his honour.

Palais des Nations, the headquarters of the United Nations

CERN

The European Centre for Nuclear Research (CERN; tours available, reservations needed; www.cern.ch), on Geneva's northern outskirts, is the world centre for particle physics research. Guides explain CERN's work and take visitors to the antimatter factory or the particle accelerators.

A mythical spot in Geneva is the **Bains des Paquis** (Paquis baths), which date from 1932 and were recently renovated. This natural swimming pool is built at the port on the right side.

After crossing the **Mon-Repos** and **Perle du Lac** parks bordering the lake, you will arrive at the **Botanical Garden**. This ensemble brings together greenhouses filled with tropical plants, a pond filled with aquatic vegetation, an arboretum, a rock garden covered in mountain plants and an aviary.

GENEVA'S MUSEUMS

Geneva is a very active city, both culturally and artistically, and is particularly rich in museums, foundations and galleries. At the **Musée d'Histoire Naturelle** (Museum of Natural History; Tue–Sun 10am–5pm; free), you can traverse 2km (about 1 mile) of corridors on several levels, viewing some 3,000 species of mammal and marine life. The birds are accompanied by samples of birdsong.

The most important of Geneva's museums is the **Musée d'Art et d'Histoire ❸** (Museum of Art and History; Tue–Sun 11am–6pm; free). The painting department contains works by Dutch, Flemish, French and Swiss masters. The most precious work here is the altarpiece from St Peter's Cathedral, painted by Konrad Witz in 1444. Entitled *La Pêche Miraculeuse* (The Miracle of the Fishes), this painting is the first in art history to represent an identifiable landscape. It features Christ walking on the waters of the port of Geneva.

Important temporary exhibitions organised by the Museum of Art and History are presented at the **Musée Rath** (see page 106).

The **Centre d'Art Contemporain** (http://centre.ch; Tue–Sun 11am–6pm) offers temporary exhibitions of new experimental artists, performances and also film screenings. The former factory for the Geneva Society for Physics Instruments is now the headquarters for the **Musée d'Art Moderne et Contemporain (MAMCO)** (www.mamco.ch; Tue–Fri noon–6pm, Sat–Sun 11am–6pm), with 4,000 sq m (13,120 sq ft) of surface area devoted to widely varying exhibitions.

The **Patek Philippe Museum** (near the Plainpalais at 7 rue des Vieux-Grenadiers; www.patekmuseum.com; Tue–Fri 2–6pm, Sat 10am–6pm) displays a collection of watches dating back to the 16th century and has a workshop where you can see a master watchmaker in action.

Courtyard at the Museum of Art and History

VAUD AND LAKE GENEVA

In the canton of **Vaud**, the most populous in western Switzerland, French is spoken, mixed with the rural dialect of the region. Two mountain ranges, the Alps and the Jura, surround Vaud, providing wide variations of landscapes and climate. To the south, the Lake of Geneva *(Lac Léman)* – the largest of the Alpine lakes – has two-thirds of its waters in Swiss territory and the other third in France. Lake Geneva has always fascinated artists, poets and composers. As peaceful as it seems most of the time, with sailing boats, steamers and motorboats, elegant swans and carefree ducks, this miniature ocean can unleash the occasional tempest throwing huge waves against the shores of the crescent-shaped lake.

In summer, vacationers and Vaud natives politely compete for space on the café terraces; small glasses of the local white wine are emptied as fast as they can be refilled.

LA CÔTE

With a view across Lake Geneva to the French Alps, the villages of **La Côte** are dotted along the 60km (37 miles) of lake shore from the edge of Geneva eastwards to the busy university and commercial city of Lausanne. If you drive from town to town, take the lake road that is parallel to the water rather than the motorway further inland. Beyond Nyon begins the wine-growing region of La Côte. You can follow the signposted Route du Vignoble (Route of the Vineyards) up gently terraced hillsides. Some highlights to visit along the coast:

Coppet ❸❾ evokes the memory of a great writer, Germaine Necker, better known as Madame de Staël. Her father, Jacques Necker, a Genevan banker who was named Director General of Finance under Louis XVI, acquired the **château** (today a museum) in 1784. When Madame de Staël fled

Napoleon's Paris in 1803, she exiled herself to Coppet, where she surrounded herself with a court of her own: Benjamin Constant, Madame de Récamier and Chateaubriand. One of her friends reported that 'more wit is dispensed in one day at Coppet than in one year anywhere else in the world'.

In the town centre of **Nyon** is the **Musée Romain** (Roman Museum; www.mrn.ch; summer Tue–Sun 10am–5pm; winter Tue–Sun 2–5pm), which houses the ruins of a Roman basilica, as well as remains and artifacts of Roman life in the area.

The five-towered **château** (www.chateaudenyon.ch; Tue–Sun Apr–Oct 10am–5pm, Nov–Mar 2–5pm) of Nyon served as a bastion for the dukes of Savoy, who expanded their domain from the other side of the lake. In the courtyard, a Romanesque mosaic recalls that Nyon was founded by Julius Caesar around 45 BC. The château contains a collection of pretty Nyon porcelain, which dates from the late 18th and early 19th

Lavaux, the wine-growing region beside Lake Geneva

Fireworks at the Paléo Festival

centuries. Near the château, on the rue Maupertuis, the vestiges of a Roman basilica from the 1st century ad stand next to a small museum full of Roman objects found here and elsewhere in the region.

In April, Nyon welcomes the international documentary film festival Visions du Réel, while in July, during the **Paléo Festival** (www.paleo.ch) a wave of musical madness descends on Nyon. This French-speaking Woodstock (previously the Nyon Folk Festival) brings together many musical styles and trends.

Rolle is endowed with a 13th-century castle on the banks of the lake. The inhabitants of Bern, who invaded the canton of Vaud in the 16th century, burned it down twice.

Morges makes its reputation in spring, when the annual Tulip Festival is held here. No less than 300,000 of these flowers are displayed in Independence Park, near the lake. Before the construction of the railway, Morges was an important port for the ferrymen of the lake.

The imposing **château** on the port was erected in the 13th century by Louis I of Savoy; it now contains the **Military Museum of Vaud** (daily July–Aug 10am–5pm, Mar–Nov Tue–Fri 10am–noon, 1.30–5pm, Sat–Sun 1.30–5pm), displaying uniforms, flags, arms and 8,000 tiny leaden soldiers. In the Grand-Rue, the museum inside the 16th-century **Alexis Forel house** has a collection of furniture, porcelain and glass, as well as antique dolls and toys.

LAUSANNE

There is always something happening in this prosperous city, capital of the canton of Vaud and headquarters of the International Olympic Committee (IOC). Cosmopolitan **Lausanne**'s  attractions include ballet (the Béjart company), classical music concerts, operas, jazz, theatre, cinema (the Swiss *cinemathèque*) and fairs.

The history of *Lousonna* goes back to Roman times, when it was an important crossroads for trade. An episcopal city since the beginning of the 12th century, Lausanne grew in economic importance over the course of the Middle Ages. In 1537, the Academy (later to be a university) was created, giving this religious and commercial centre an intellectual bent. Since 1874, Lausanne has been the seat of the Federal Tribunal, the highest judicial body in the Swiss Confederation.

Roman columns at Nyon's Place des Marronniers

Ouchy, situated on the banks of Lake Geneva, is the liveliest part of town, with parks, cafés, a château (now a hotel) and the Olympic Museum (see page 117). From the port, large white steamers leave for Vevey, Montreux, Evian, Thonon, Morges, Nyon and Geneva.

A stone's throw from Ouchy, and also located on the lake's edge, is the

Vidy Theatre. This hosts productions (sometimes in their European premiere) by such well-known directors as Peter Brook and Robert Wilson.

To leave Ouchy for the **place Saint-François**, a commercial square built around a 13th-century church, take what the locals call the recently rebuilt and extended *métro* between Ouchy and the old town). From Saint-François, you can follow the boutique-lined rue de Bourg to the rue Caroline, before crossing the Bessières bridge.

There is no need to describe the way to the **cathedral**; it is impossible to miss as it looms before you. Built in Burgundian Gothic style and finished in 1275, the cathedral retains some remarkable vestiges of the 13th century, including some lovely **choir stalls** and a **rose window** in the transept. An ancient tradition is still observed in the sanctuary: every night, between 10pm and 2am, a crier announces the hours to the city from the top of the church tower.

The old episcopal palace, located next door to the cathedral, currently holds the **Musée Historique de Lausanne** (Historical Museum of Lausanne; Tue–Thu 11am–6pm, Fri–Sun 11am–5pm; also Mon July–Aug). Temporary exhibitions are also shown here.

Covered staircases descend from the cathedral to the **place de la Palud**, which has hosted an outdoor market since the Middle Ages (now held on Wednesday and Saturday mornings). This does not detract from the solemn dignity of Lausanne's 17th-century **Hôtel de Ville** (town hall), with its attractive ensemble of arches, clock tower and gargoyles.

The town has a dozen or so museums devoted to subjects ranging from the history of the Olympics to that of pipe-smokers. But the most original museum in Switzerland may be the **Collection of Primitive Art** (*Art Brut*; www.artbrut.ch; Tue–Sun 11am–6pm, daily July–Aug 11am–6pm), which is housed in a 13th-century castle, near the palace of Beaulieu. This dazzling collection of art by untrained artists, including psychiatric patients, was founded by the artist Jean Dubuffet.

North of Lausanne is the **Hermitage Foundation** (Tue–Sun 10am–6pm, Thu until 9pm), with a view of the lake and the historic town centre; temporary painting exhibitions are held here.

The **Musée de l'Elysée** (18 avenue de l'Elysée; www. elysee.ch; Tue–Sun 11am–6pm, Thu until 8pm) occupies an appealing 19th-century residence. It specialises in photography, inviting visitors to trace the history of the art, from the daguerrotype to ultra-modern techniques. It also offers a rich programme of frequently changing exhibitions.

The **Olympic Museum** (1 quai d'Ouchy; www.olympic.org; May–Oct daily 9am–6pm, Oct–Apr Tue–Sun 10am–6pm) has a detailed display on the history of sports and the Olympic movement.

The sculpture Ouverture au Monde in Ouchy, by Angelo Duarte

THE VAUD RIVIERA

This region extends from the suburbs of Lausanne to the eastern edge of Lake Geneva. Villette, Epesses and Saint-Saphorin are typical wine-growing villages, depicted in literature by C.F. Ramuz, a writer from the Vaud region. Whatever your method of transport (boat, train or car), the landscapes of the Lavaux are something to see.

Just before Vevey, at Corseaux, a white wall draws your eye: it is the **Villa Le Corbusier**, designed in the early 1920s by Le Corbusier and Pierre Jeanneret.

Chocolate and wine are the twin foundations of **Vevey**'s fortune. In fact, the largest building in town, a glass structure with concave walls, is the worldwide centre for Nestlé, the multinational food manufacturer. And viticulture, the region's other important resource, has given rise to the Fête des Vignerons (Vineyard Festival), celebrated every 25 years or so since the 16th century (the last one was in 1999). This popular

CHOCOLATE AND CHEESE

Want to combine three of Switzerland's most famous activities (tasting cheese, sampling chocolate and taking a scenic train ride) into one adventure? The Chocolate Train takes travellers in either a Pullman car or panoramic train from Montreux to the popular cheese town of Gruyères and then on to the Nestlé-Cailler chocolate factory in Broc. At Gruyères, you will tour a cheese-making facility and taste its famous cheese. You will also be able to tour the castle. Then, you continue on to Broc, where the famous Swiss version of Nestlé chocolate is made. After a brief video and tour, the visit ends in the tasting room, filled with samples of each Cailler chocolate variety and complemented by tasting tips and tidbits on the different chocolates. For more information, go to www.myswitzerland.raileurope.com.

festival brings together thousands of willing participants from the region, creating a splendid spectacle.

The old town is a wonderful place to explore. Among the 18th- and 19th-century houses are squares with many fine old fountains.

A cog train goes from Vevey to **Les Pleiades**, a belvedere with a panoramic vista

Villa Le Corbusier

at 1,360m (4,460ft) above sea level. Here you can take in the entire lake with the Alps behind it. Halfway up, **Blonay** is both the site of a 12th-century castle and the end of the line for a small tourist railway (the Blonay-Chamby line; www.blonay-chamby.ch) whose steam locomotives and cars date from the early 20th century.

Far above the vineyards and orchards of Vevey, a funicular climbs to the next vista, **Mont-Pèlerin**. Don't miss the panoramic tower, the 'Plein Ciel' (Open Sky), with a 360º view of the whole lake region.

Near the far end of the lake, the fin-de-siècle palaces of **Montreux** ㊶ attract tourists all year round. Vladimir Nabokov, author of Lolita, spent his final days in one of these hotels. Montreux owes its Mediterranean atmosphere to a microclimate, which favours all kinds of blossoming plants. The town is also the setting for international shows such as the prestigious Montreux Jazz Festival (July; www.montreuxjazz.com), the Musical September classical music festival and the Festival of Laughter (December). The casino, Switzerland's first, looks out on the lakefront, adding to this resort's appeal.

Narcissus field at Les Pleiades with the Alps in the background

The **old town**, tucked into the hillside, also charms, with its 18th-century stone houses, antique shops and artisans' boutiques.

A mountain train makes the climb up to **Rochers-de-Naye** (www.mob.ch), at an elevation of more than 2,000m (6,560ft), passing through orchards, pastures and forests: the views along the way are stupendous. The site is also a haven for hikers, rock-climbers and skydivers.

If you like your landscapes as seen through a window, board the unique Panoramic Express. A brainchild of the Montreux-Oberland Bernois (MOB; www.mob.ch), this train offers unbeatable views over Lake Geneva before continuing on to Gruyères, Château-d'Oex, Rougemont, Gstaad and Zweisimmen with connections for Interlaken and Lucerne.

East of Montreux, the most celebrated of all Swiss châteaux, the **Château de Chillon** ㊷ (www.chillon.ch; daily Apr–Sept 9am–6pm, Mar and Oct 9.30am–5pm, Nov–Feb 10am–4pm), is an austere feudal fortress, oddly wedged between the lake and the railway line. The great rock of Chillon, projecting out over Lake Geneva, was always a natural stronghold from which to guard the major Saint Bernard road linking Rome to its northern provinces. There were probably fortifications on the spot since ancient times, and a rudimentary château, which belonged to the bishops of Sion, was later fortified and enlarged by the dukes of Savoy. In 1536, after a three-day siege, the fortress fell into the hands of the Bernese.

FOUR RESORTS IN VAUD

The resorts of Vaud have developed modern infrastructures without losing their Old-World character. It is this balance that accounts for their popularity and appeal.

Château-d'Oex (960m/3,150ft; www.chateau-doex.ch). A pleasant village snuggled into the welcoming valley of the Pays d'Enhaut, it is ideal for family vacations. The interesting Musée du Pays d'Enhaut showcases the arts, crafts and history of the region. You can also visit Etivaz to watch local craftsmen make the cheese of the same name. At the end of January, one of the most famous international airshows takes place here, bringing together over 100 hot-air balloons.

Les Diablerets (1,150m/3,770ft; www.diablerets.ch). This family-style resort occupies a beautiful Alpine site. A cable car makes three stops on the way to the top of one of Switzerland's most impressive glaciers – Les Diablerets (3,000m/9,840ft), where you can ski all year round, hike on the glacier, ride the Alpine Coaster or go for a dog sled ride.

Leysin (1,250m/4,100ft; www.leysin.ch). This spectacular sunny spot, facing the Dents du Midi and the Mont Blanc mountain range, has beginning and intermediate-level ski slopes. Each January, Leysin plays host to the European Snowboard Championship.

Villars-sur-Ollon (1,250m/4,100ft; www.villars.ch). A family resort full of activity at weekends, with sports ranging from downhill and cross-country skiing and skating, to horseback riding, swimming, tennis and golf. Gryon (1,110m/3,640ft) is a continuation of and complement to Villars. Gryon has preserved its traditional character, and its abundant fauna and flora make it an unmissable gem.

FRIBOURG, NEUCHÂTEL AND THE JURA

These three neighbouring cantons have very distinct characteristics and strong personalities of their own.

FRIBOURG

The hilly terrain of **Fribourg** ㊸ has made it a town in three dimensions, built at once along the Sarine river (*Saane* in German) and on a cliff above it. What first strikes the visitor's eye is the harmony between the wild gorges and the marvellous Gothic buildings.

Founded in 1157 by Duke Berchtold IV of Zähringen, Fribourg joined the Confederation in 1481. When the Reformation

Historic Fribourg, on the Sarine River

seized Bern, Fribourg resisted. Today, it remains steadfastly Catholic, with its churches, seminaries and theological bookshops. Fribourg is also a bilingual town. Zähringen Bridge offers the classic view of the river, the 13th- and 15th-century ramparts on the steep hillside, and the old covered bridge linking the banks of the Sarine. There has been a bridge at this point ever since the 13th century.

Like most of the historical buildings in Fribourg, the **Cathédrale Saint-Nicolas** is made of sandstone. Age, weather and pollution have left their mark on the structure. The Gothic statues that frame the main portal are copies; the originals are in the Catholic University and the Museum of Art and History. Inside the cathedral, note the striking sculptural ensemble *Entombment of Christ* (1433) in the Chapel of the Holy Sepulchre.

Another important architectural work is the **Eglise de Cordeliers**, founded in the 13th century by Franciscan monks. Among its highlights are the oak choir stalls (1280), a fine altarpiece (1480) above the main altar and, in one of the side chapels, a triptych of sculpted and gilded wood (1513).

The **Musée d'Art et d'Histoire** (Art and History Museum; www.fr.ch; Tue–Sun 11am–6pm, Thu until 8pm) is installed in the Hôtel Ratzé, a splendid Renaissance residence; part of it also occupies a nearby 19th-century slaughterhouse. The eclectic collections found in this museum are based on the past of Fribourg and its immediate environs.

Next to the Art and History Museum, the space devoted to the works of Fribourg native Jean Tinguely and his companion Niki de Saint-Phalle is very interesting and a definite mustsee (www.fr.ch; Wed–Sun 11am–6pm, Thu until 8pm).

The **Hôtel de Ville** (town hall) is notable for its great sloping roof and its covered ceremonial staircase and turreted clock tower which date back to the early 16th century.

AROUND FRIBOURG

Murten (Morat). This bilingual town is a marvel of perfectly preserved old houses with deep arcades and overhanging roofs. You can climb up to the medieval towers and ramparts to survey the tile roofs, the town's little lake and the countryside. Also worthy of note here is the 13th-century castle and the solid Bern Gate, with its bell and belfry. In summer, some excursion boats go from the Murten lake to Biel and Neuchâtel.

Avenches ㊹. *Aventicum* was the capital of Roman Helvetia. Around AD 260, it was sacked by Alemanni tribesmen, and no one knows what happened to its 20,000 inhabitants. In the Middle Ages a new town was founded on the same site, but its prosperity never approached that of the ancient capital.

At the far end of the rue Centrale, visit the **amphitheatre**, where 8,000 spectators could gather to watch gladiators in the Roman era. Today, it is used for open-air operas. Above the main entrance, a medieval tower now houses the **Roman Museum** (www.aventicum.org; Tue–Sun Apr–Sept 10am–5pm, Oct–Mar 2–5pm), whose collections are supplied by ongoing archaeological digs. Around Avenches there are several other Roman ruins to visit, including a theatre and parts of the ancient wall.

Dividing line

The towns and villages that lie along the German/French linguistic divide are on the so-called Barrière de Rösti. This 'barrier' between the two regions is named after the popular Swiss dish made from potatoes that originates from the German part of Switzerland.

Payerne. This small town in the Broye valley is home to the **Abbatiale**, the largest Romanesque church in the country and the only remaining vestige of an important Benedictine abbey. After the Reformation, this remarkable building was abandoned. But more than a half-century of restorations have revealed

The picturesque Murten

architectural elements from the 11th century, such as the majestic columns supporting the vaulted ceiling.

Gruyères ㊺. This large, fortified medieval village, high on a hilltop, draws tourists from the world over. Arrive early in summer. The **castle** (www.chateau-gruyeres.ch; daily Apr–Oct 9am–6pm, Nov–Mar 10am–5pm), built by the counts of Gruyères in the 12th century, is definitely worth a visit, if only for the view from the battlements. The worn steps of the spiral staircase lead you to the well-preserved state rooms and private apartments.

Don't leave Gruyères without tasting some of its specialities: fondue and meringue, raspberries and blueberries, all served with the thick, smooth cream particular to this region. At the foot of the hill, a model dairy shows you the secrets involved in making the famous Gruyère cheese (daily June–Sept 9am–7pm, Oct–May 9am–6pm).

Bulle, 11km (7 miles) from Gruyères, is the site of a fine 13th-century castle (was due to reopen in February 2012 after renovation) and the **Gruyères Museum**, which illustrates the customs of the region.

NEUCHÂTEL

The lakeside town of **Neuchâtel** ⑯ has a long intellectual tradition, which lives on in its university, its schools and its specialised institutes. The town has belonged successively to the Holy Roman Empire, the dukes of Burgundy and the kings of Prussia. It was not until 1857 that Prussia officially recognised the independence of the canton, even though it had been a Confederation member since 1815. The 'tick-tock' of official Swiss time is emitted by the Chronometric Observatory of Neuchâtel, the research centre for the clockmaking industry.

The old crossroads of the Croix du Marché, a few streets in from the port, contains buildings and fountains constructed between the 16th and 18th centuries. The most original structure in this area is the **Maison des Halles** (1575), which was once a covered market.

The town is dominated by a monumental group of medieval buildings, where once church, prison and government shared a fortified enclosure. Inside the **Collégiale** (collegiate church), a remarkable sculpture immortalises the counts of Neuchâtel. The castle (12th–16th centuries) is now the seat of the cantonal government. The top of the prison tower (15th century) commands the best view of the town and the lake. To the west, on rue Saint-Nicolas, the **Musée d'Ethnographie** (Ethnographic Museum; Tue–Sun 10am–5pm) has several good collections relating to Ancient Egypt, Africa and Oceania. The **Musée d'Art et d'Histoire**, on Esplanade Léopold-Robert close to the port, is dedicated to Swiss artists and to religious paintings of the Middle Ages. It brings together rare Swiss ceramics, 16th-century watches, armour, coins and medallions (Tue–Sun 11am–6pm).

AROUND NEUCHÂTEL LAKE

The charming town of **Grandson** was the scene of a famous triumph in Swiss history: the 1476 defeat of Charles the Bold, Duke of Burgundy, by Confederate troops. At the castle, you can see a re-enactment of this event with lead soldiers. Climb the ramparts (13th century) to visit the museum of antique cars, featuring Greta Garbo's 1923 Rolls-Royce.

Yverdon-les-Bains, known for its mineral baths since Roman times, is once again flourishing as a spa. In the centre of town, a 13th-century castle houses the municipal museum. One room is devoted to Pestalozzi, a pioneer of pedagogy, who ran a school here in the 19th century.

Neuchâtel's Collégiale

A variety of architectural styles coexist in the walled town of **Estavayer-le-Lac**, located on the south bank of Neuchâtel Lake. The Château de Chenaux dates from the 13th century, while the Saint-Laurent church in the heart of town is mainly of late Gothic style. A most surprising attraction is the **Museum of Frogs** (www.museedes grenouilles.ch; July–Aug daily 10am–noon, 2–5pm; Mar–June and Sept–Oct Tue–Sun 10am–noon, 2–5pm; Nov–Feb Sat–Sun 2–5pm), filled with over 100 stuffed frogs in surreal poses.

THE JURA

French-speaking **Jura**, established in 1979, is the baby among Swiss cantons. The Jurassic range links Geneva to Basel, accompanying the French border on one side and stretching across half a dozen Swiss cantons on the other. It is a zone of meadows, lakes and fir forests interspersed with the region's typical dwellings, enclosed in dry-stone walls. Life is harsh in this sparsely populated region, where for centuries watchmaking, practised at home, was the economic mainstay. For the tourist seeking peace and beauty, the Jura is a great discovery.

The magnificent village of **Romainmôtier**, tucked into an idyllic valley, takes its name from the monastery (*moûtier* in old French) founded here around AD 450 by Saint Romain. The church, dating from the 10th and 11th centuries, is absolutely remarkable. You can still see, on the floor in front of the organ, the traces of two earlier churches. The frescoes are from the 12th and 13th centuries; the Romanesque sculptures represent demons and wonders of the medieval world. In the choir, there is a sculpted 7th-century ambon (an early kind of pulpit). The 14th-century clock tower and the 15th-century priory are all that remains of the monastery.

The main attraction of **La Chaux-de-Fonds** ㊼, a town of 40,000 inhabitants devoted to clockmaking, is the 'Man and Time' exhibition at the **Musée d'Horlogerie du Locle** (International Clock making Museum; www.mhl-monts.ch; May–Oct Tue–Sun

Early Le Corbusier

Native son Le Corbusier realised some of his first architectural projects in La Chaux-de-Fonds. The fruits of this era include the Fallet villa (1906, decorated in Jurassian Art Nouveau), the Jacquemet villa (1908) and the Stotzer villa (1908). The architect's character can be clearly seen in the mature design of the Villa Turque (1917). Some time after these projects were completed, Le Corbusier moved to Paris.

Castle and collegiate church of Estavayer-le-Lac, Neuchâtel Lake

10am–5pm, Nov–Apr Tue–Sun 2pm–5pm). It is unique, both architecturally – the museum is entirely underground – and in its collection. With over 3,000 timepieces on display, from sundials to hourglasses to modern chronometers, it is the most important museum of its kind in the world. Note the 17th-century enamelled watches.

To the north of the town begin the forests and pastures of the **Franches-Montagnes**. This peaceful region's main activity is the raising of horses. **Saignelégier**, the county seat, welcomes important events each year, such as the Horse Fair and Market (in summer) and the dogsled races (in winter).

The Doubs river, originating in France, encloses the town of **Saint-Ursanne**, where pink, white and ochre-coloured stone houses vie for space on the riverbank. After crossing the narrow, swaybacked bridge, you enter the walled town, where life revolves around the **Collégiale** (collegiate church). Like the village, the church takes its name from Saint Ursinicus, an Irish pilgrim of the 12th century, who lived in the Doubs valley.

WHAT TO DO

SPORTS

Downhill skiing. Whether you're a champion or a beginner, Switzerland remains the homeland of this sport, offering the best possible conditions of comfort and safety, not to mention the most beautiful landscapes.

Nearly 200 villages and towns are equipped for downhill skiing: Valais offers a wide choice of resorts, including Zermatt, Crans-Montana, Saas-Fee or Champéry, from which you can reach the Portes du Soleil (650km/400 miles of slopes, with 230 mechanical lifts). The Grisons mountains also have superb skiing, with St Moritz, Pontresina, Davos and Klosters, as well as Flims and Laax, with their Alpenarena. The Alps of Vaud, the Jura and central Switzerland also offer wonderful ski slopes.

In most regions the season lasts from late November through to early April, but conditions vary according to the year and the resort. The high seasons (when prices and crowds are at their height) are Christmas, Easter and February. Outside these times, you can get better package deals. Throughout winter, Swiss ski schools organise group courses taught by qualified instructors, who will also give private lessons.

Before hitting the slopes, don't forget to bring sunblock and sunglasses to protect you from the blinding glare. Be cautious: regulate your speed according to your physical condition and level of expertise in order to avoid having to call the security patrols (efficient and well-equipped though they are).

Snowboarding. Snowboarders will not be disappointed with what's on offer here. Besides the slopes that can be shared with skiers, many resorts are setting aside areas with jumps, obstacle courses and a young, 'cool' atmosphere (Grindelwald First, Laax and Adelboden Hahnenmoos, to name three).

An adventurous skier tackling the slopes

Snowblading. This recent addition to the world of winter sports, practised on shorter skis without poles, is wonderfully exhilarating. If you don't dare go it alone at first, many ski schools offer snowblading courses.

Cross-country skiing (*Langlauf* in German). This sport has come back into fashion in recent years. Glide through the wooded countryside or follow a stream or river, stopping along the way for a picnic or lunch on a restaurant terrace. The tracks are groomed and ranked according to difficulty. Some resorts have up to 100km (60 miles) of tracks, and new ones are being opened each year. The Jura, Engadine and Appenzell are particularly popular locations.

Skating. Most resorts have natural or artificial rinks open throughout the winter. Skate hire and lessons are available.

Curling. This sport, which involves sliding heavy polished blocks of stone across a rectangular track of ice, can be

SLED RUNS

For a thrill of a lifetime, consider three downhill sled runs in the St Moritz area. At the Cresta Run, the rider hurtles headfirst down an ice track on a skeleton sled at speeds of up to 140kph (87mph). Those who would prefer to leave the driving to a professional, might consider the St Moritz/Celerina Olympia Bobrun. Here, riders race on a real bobsled course with a professional driver in front and brakeman at the back. Visit the St Moritz tourist website at www.stmoritz.ch or call 081 837 3333 for more information on these two runs.

For a slower descent, consider the Preda-Bergun toboggan run just outside St Moritz in Bergun. On this track, riders travel at their leisure on wooden sleds for a fraction of the cost. Contact the Bergun tourist office at 081 407 1152 for more information.

practised in many places in Switzerland. Open-air and covered tracks are available.

Skydiving and hang-gliding. The Swiss terrain is very well suited to these adventure sports (at Lenzerheide, Rigi, Salève and St Moritz).

Summer skiing. In resorts near glaciers, such as Les Diablerets, Verbier, Zermatt, Saas-Fee and Pontresina, you can easily ski all morning and swim all afternoon. Many of them operate lifts and cable cars all summer.

Rock-climbing. A professional guide and adequate equipment are of crucial

Hiking in the mountains

importance for this sport. Rescuers often bewail the carelessness of people who dress as if for a tennis match to make their way over difficult, often unpredictable rockfaces. The best option for newcomers is to take a climbing course.

Mountain trekking. Trekking is less dangerous than climbing, but it is still important to take precautions and to be well equipped, with good boots and the right clothing. Be careful not to leave the marked paths. For greater safety, get detailed maps from the local tourist office. The Swiss Alpine Club also has a list of huts available in the mountains.

Hiking. Switzerland has about 62,000km (38,750 miles) of marked hiking trails. Wherever you go, you will see yellow signs that designate the trails and indicate the journey time to the next checkpoint. It is easy to find books, leaflets, apps or maps suggesting the most attractive hikes in the region.

Swimming. Switzerland's lakefronts, beaches and creeks are available to everyone. Most cities and resorts have beaches as well as swimming pools, not to mention the thermal baths at resorts such as Bad Ragaz, Leukerbad, Yverdon, Ovronnaz and Scuol.

Windsurfing. You can hire equipment to experience this ever-more-popular sport; instructors will help you get yourself up and afloat.

Waterskiing. This expensive sport is practised at some major lakeside resorts, although on some lakes it is forbidden for environmental reasons.

Sailing. Hardly a weekend goes by in summer without a major regatta taking place somewhere in Switzerland. You can hire yachts or paddleboats on most lakes. You will need a permit

Wakeboarding in Fribourg

to navigate a sailboat with a sail larger than 14 sq m (46 sq ft), but you can content yourself with a small dinghy or a canoe. Beware the sudden gusts of wind that often arise on the lakes.

Fishing. Lakes and rivers are restocked every year (with trout, char and pike). The local police station issues permits for a day, week or year, and will notify you of the regulations, which vary from one spot to the next.

Swiss wrestling

Folklore and sport meet in the ancient tradition of Swiss wrestling *(Hosenlupf)*. The wrestlers, wearing special leggings, clash grimly until one of them throws his adversary into the sawdust, all according to the strictest rules. There is fighting of a very different kind in the Valais region: 'combats of the queens' (cow fights) attract crowds every Sunday in spring.

Golf. There are about 60 courses throughout Switzerland. In the Alps, every possibility for building a golf course seems to have been explored (in St Moritz, you can play golf all winter on a frozen lake). If you belong to a golf club in your own country, you will usually be admitted to one here for a small fee.

Tennis. Many of the resorts and most big cities have tennis courts, although the city facilities are often overrun with people. Lessons are available. Every summer, the Swiss Open, the Gstaad International Championship, attracts the world's best players.

Horse riding. There are stables and riding schools on the outskirts of major cities, as well as in vacation spots. Contact the Swiss tourist office (see page 177) or ask a travel agent about the particulars of an equestrian vacation.

Cycling and mountain biking. You can hire a bike at a railway station and take it back to any other designated bike-hire station. Switzerland's terrain makes it an ideal place for mountain biking. Ask at the local tourist office for recommended routes; detailed maps are available as well.

SHOPPING

Cheeses, chocolate and cuckoo clocks: these are the first items that shopping in Switzerland brings to mind, but there are many other possibilities. Luxury goods, such as furs, watches and jewels, are the best deals available. On the other hand, many everyday articles may seem expensive here, due to the strength of the Swiss franc. But the quality of the items is rarely in question, as the Swiss themselves are demanding consumers. Salespeople are generally courteous and efficient.

Look out for good buys during the annual sale periods of January–February and July–August. No taxes need be added: the price on the label is the price you pay.

WHERE TO SHOP

Zurich and Geneva are known all over the world for their chic boutiques, as are Basel and Bern and resorts such as Gstaad and St Moritz. If your budget doesn't allow you the occasional splurge, you can find reasonable buys in department stores, where prices seldom vary from one canton to the next.

WHAT TO BUY

Liquor. Fruit brandies *(eaux-de-vie)* are easy to transport and make excellent souvenirs or gifts: they include apple, kirsch (cherry), marc (made from champagne), pear, plum and gentian.

Antiques. Whatever you're looking for, you can find it here. Luxury antiques shops and secondhand dealers are everywhere. To find silver and old jewellery or any other precious object, go to the auctions held in Zurich or Geneva. And don't turn up your nose at street fairs and flea markets, where it's always possible to discover a real find.

Art. Art galleries abound, in small towns and big cities alike. Specialists in the field make sure that Swiss prices remain

Handmade Swiss chocolate

competitive with foreign ones, and merchants are glad to ship paintings and sculptures anywhere in the world.

Cheese. Merchants can tell you which cheeses will survive the trip home and will wrap them accordingly (see page 142).

Chocolate. Switzerland produces what is easily the largest variety of chocolates in the world. Milk chocolate, particularly, is of the highest quality. You will find an amazing choice of truffles in luxury chocolate shops.

Embroidery. St-Gallen has made its reputation in the world of embroidery; look especially for napkins, tablecloths, blouses and handkerchiefs.

Jewellery. Jewels and gold are of the highest quality here. Gaze at the sumptuous window displays on major shopping streets, but don't neglect tiny stores in side streets of old towns.

Knives. The Swiss Army Knife – a little tool kit that fits in your pocket – can include more than 30 features, from a corkscrew to a miniature saw. It can take on a myriad of tasks.

Watches and clocks. From the 'disposable' watch to the finest timepiece, the choice here is immense. You can rest assured that whatever model you choose will come with an international guarantee. If you want something fancier than a Swatch, choose a Rolex, an Audemars Piguet or a Blancpain.

As for cuckoo clocks, they do really exist, in every size, in department stores and souvenir boutiques. If the little bird who chirps the hours isn't serious enough for you, perhaps a pendulum clock from Neuchâtel will tempt you instead.

Souvenirs. Some local choices include cowbells, collectable dolls and yodelling records, but there are also fossils or rocks from the Alps, crafted objects from the *Heimatwerk* (home-craft) boutiques, wooden toys, bowls, plates, music boxes, copper, pewter, painted Easter eggs and landscapes or silhouettes cut out of paper.

ENTERTAINMENT

Swiss cities have a livelier nightlife than you might imagine. Even in relatively isolated places, it is not unusual to find a disco, an outdoor dance or a concert. But in a country where work often begins at 7am, night crawlers are a rare sight. Nightclubs that offer floor shows and orchestras exist only in the bigger cities. Elsewhere, entertainment is often limited to a piano player, but there is a certain charm in the simpler pleasures Switzerland has to offer, like sharing a good bottle

---

Traditional music

During festivals, or in market places, you will often hear the sombre sound of the alphorn, a curious wind instrument of astonishing size. Another unique Swiss sound, yodelling, may be encountered in restaurants in German-speaking areas, as well as at festivals.

Curtain call: the elaborate Chamber Theatre in Bern

of wine by a fire in a mountain chalet, or taking a 'dancing cruise' on a lake.

International tours by important musical artists invariably include a few Swiss cities among their stops. Swiss chamber orchestras and symphonies, such as the famous Orchestre de la Suisse Romande, often give concerts. Look into the possibility of hearing medieval music in a castle courtyard, or an organ recital in an old church. There are also frequent music festivals in the area, the most famous of which is held in Lucerne in August.

Opera and dance performances are easy to find in Zurich, Geneva, Basel, Bern, Lausanne and St-Gallen.

Jazz, both traditional and avant-garde, is not neglected either, but all the concerts to be heard around the country during the year are just warm-ups for the Montreux Festival.

Swiss theatre is well regarded everywhere; good local troupes alternate with foreign companies on tour. Every genre is represented, and the productions are of the highest quality.

CHILDREN'S SWITZERLAND

Tobogganing is a favourite activity for children of all ages and can be found in most mountain resorts. Some areas have illuminated pistes for night runs, such as at Grindelwald in the Bernese Oberland. Many resorts also have skating rinks. In the warmer months, children will enjoy the hiking and biking trails, as well as play areas.

Switzerland's many lakes provide a multitude of fun activities during the spring and summer, including boat rides and hiring a paddle boat. Most cities have public swimming beaches, some with water slides, as in Geneva. Also, near Montreux, there is a large water park in Le Bouveret.

There are festivals all year round, and most will have activities for children. Some of the larger festivals have rides and games, including the *Fêtes de Genève* in August. Basel's *Fasnacht* is one of the most famous festivals in the country.

Switzerland has two of the best zoos in Europe at Basel and Zurich (www.zoo.ch). Basel's, the largest in the country, is particularly known for the successful breeding of endangered species (see page 42).

There are also a number of museums that will interest children, including the Jean Tinguely Museum in Basel (see page 44) with its machines and gadgets, the Verkehrshaus transport museum in Lucerne (see page 70) with its aeroplanes and locomotives, and the Swissminiatur museum near Lugano (see page 93) with its miniature models of all things Swiss.

Tobogganing fun

CALENDAR OF EVENTS

Quite apart from the international cultural festivals in the major cities, there is no Swiss village, no matter how small, that does not put on at least one festival a year. Regional tourist offices publish annual brochures listing all the celebrations planned for the region.

January. Celebrations ring in the New Year. Horse races in the snow in St Moritz and Arosa; Vogel-Gryff Day in Basel; *Silvesterklausen* in Urnäsch, where men dress up in traditional masked costumes.

February/March. Carnival *(Fasnacht)* in Bern, Basel, Lucerne and other Catholic parts of Switzerland.

March. In Engadine, the *Chalanda März* (a children's procession of pagan origin) and the ski marathon with thousands of participants.

April. *Sechseläuten* in Zurich: bonfires with Old Man Winter, known locally as the *Böögg*; parades. Procession of weeping women in Romont.

April/May. *Landsgemeinde* in Appenzell; 'combats of the queens' (cow fights) that attract crowds every Sunday in Valais. Open House at wineries in the Geneva area.

June. Herding of cows up the Alps. International Festival in Zurich (three weeks of concerts, opera, theatre and exhibitions).

July. Jazz festival in Montreux and Paléo music festival in Nyon. East Switzerland Yodellers' Festival in Chur. Opera Festival in the amphitheatre of Avenches. 'Estival Jazz' in Lugano.

August. National Day (1 Aug). Music festivals in Lucerne and Gstaad. International film festival in Locarno. Fireworks and parades at the *Fêtes de Genève* (Geneva). Street Parade (techno music festival) in Zurich.

September. Music festivals in Montreux and Vevey. Swiss crafts fair in Lausanne. *Désalpe*, descent of the cows in Charmey (near Gruyères).

September/October. Wine harvest (*vendange* in French) festivals in Geneva, Lugano and Neuchâtel.

November. Onion market *(Zibelemärit)* in Bern (fourth Monday). Autumn fair in Basel.

December. The *Escalade* historical procession in Geneva.

EATING OUT

The Swiss like to eat and drink well and they offer their visitors enough choices to satisfy any taste, from the popular fare served in village bistros to the refined gourmet menus of world-class restaurants. Each region has its own specialities, often influenced by the traditions of the neighbouring country whose language is spoken there.

Many restaurants in Switzerland offer daily lunch specials; some will offer two or three each day. These are usually a great bargain, ranging from 15–30 Swiss francs. Many offer dinner menus which can also be good value. Some restaurants close on Sundays and during August, when much of the country is on holiday. Service is usually included but it is customary to tip if you feel the service was exceptional service (5 percent). In most resort towns, restaurants are located in the many hotels.

FONDUES AND CHEESES

A fondue is more than a meal, it's a party. Guests gather around a *caquelon* (cast-iron dish) bubbling with cheese melted with white wine (and a shot of kirsch) and, armed with long fondue forks, dip in their hunks of country bread. Besides the familiar Gruyère fondue, there are creamier variants, such as the *moitié-moitié* (half-and-half), where the Gruyère is mixed with Vacherin cheese from Fribourg, or the Fribourg fondue, which is made from Vacherin alone. There are also fondues containing wild mushrooms or tomatoes.

Meaty fondues

Those who like meat might try a *fondue bourguignonne* (Burgundian fondue) or *chinoise* (Chinese fondue).

Raclette is a cousin of fondue. A half-wheel of cheese is placed in front of a heat source – traditionally a hearth – and when the cheese begins to melt, a

A sociable dish: sharing fondue in Fribourg

portion is scraped off. The cheese falls onto your plate next to a boiled potato, onions cured in vinegar and *cornichons* (tiny pickled gherkins).

Only white wine or hot tea should be drunk with fondue or *raclette*; cold drinks are said to inhibit digestion. The same is true for the delicious pastries called *malakoffs*, a kind of savoury doughnut made with Gruyère.

Cheeses. These do not make up a course in themselves, as in France, but are served as hors d'oeuvres or at late-night suppers, accompanied by baked potatoes. Emmental is a sweet cheese full of holes. Appenzell is a sharper version. The firm interior of Gruyère (*Greyerzer* in German) has only a few small holes and tastes of hazelnut. Gruyère exists in sweet, semi-salty and salty varieties. Sbrinz, a hard cheese, is served in *rebibes* (slices as thin as cigarette paper). Firm, round and strong-smelling *Tête-de-moine* (monk's head) is a Jura speciality. It is carved out, raclette-style, until it resembles a sort of fragrant mushroom. It is generally eaten in winter.

Tomme, a sweet, soft cheese from Vaud, is sometimes combined with cumin. Reblochon, a creamy cheese, is somewhat stronger. Finally, we should mention Schabziger, a herbed cheese from the canton of Glarus that smells pretty powerful. For hunger pangs, take along a *ramequin* (*Chäschüechli* in German), a small cheese pie, or some cheese toast (*Käseschnite*).

SPECIALITIES OF FRENCH SWITZERLAND

Fish. The *omble chevalier*, or knight's char, the most delicate and delicious of freshwater fish, is usually poached and served with Hollandaise sauce or melted butter. Trout and its pink-fleshed cousin salmon trout are both excellent. Perch is most often served filleted and fried, with tartar sauce and a slice of lemon. Pike is either grilled or prepared in quenelles (dumplings), while fera fillets are baked or fried.

Assiette valaisienne

Meat. French influence is obvious in the *entrecôtes* (rib steaks) and filet mignons served here. *Assiette valaisienne* (Valais assortment) is made up of fine rolled slices of dried meat and bacon, smoked ham, sausage, cheese and tiny pickles. Wonderful with rye bread and a déci of Swiss white wine.

SPECIALITIES OF ITALIAN SWITZERLAND

Piccata, pasta and pizza. In Ticino, you eat like an Italian. But risotto here is made with onions, mushrooms and cheese.

Polenta, a thick corn purée, is served as an accompaniment to meat. Enriched with cream Ticino-style, it is called *polenta grassa* and restaurants stock it by the tureen. Taste these treats in a *grotto* – often found in the most picturesque and romantic places.

SPECIALITIES OF GERMAN SWITZERLAND

Soups. *Basler Mehlsuppe* (grilled flour soup from Basel) is eaten early in the morning during Carnival season. Another favourite is *Brotsuppe* (bread soup from Lucerne).

Fish. One of the best is *fera (Felchen)*, fished from the region's many lakes. Perch *(Egli)* and trout *(Forelle)* are often raised in tanks. *Rötel*, from the Zug lake and *Äsche*, a cousin of the trout, are eaten only in late autumn and early winter.

Meat. *Geschnitzeltes Kalbfleisch* (sliced veal in cream sauce) is called *Eminćé Zurichoise* in French-Swiss. *Berner Platte* (Bern assortment) consists of beef, sausages, sauerkraut or green beans and potatoes. *Bündnerfleisch* or Grison-style meat, is raw, air-dried beef eaten in paper-thin slices at the start of meals.

Game. Game is popular from September to February, the hunting season. Roebuck *(Rehrücken)* is served with chestnuts, cranberry sauce and red cabbage. Other wild game dishes include deer *(hirsch)*, boar *(Wildschwein)* and hare *(Hase)*.

Sausages. There are at least 45 varieties of sausage, eaten boiled, fried, grilled, cold, smoked and even in salads. *Schübling* is a pork sausage and *Bratwurst mit Zwiebelsauce* is veal sausage served with an onion sauce.

Side dishes. Don't leave this region without trying the *Rösti*, or grated, grilled potatoes. *Spätzli*, boiled pasta dumplings, are served with meat and game.

Desserts. Fruit pies are eaten for dessert or as snacks. No one can resist the *Zuger Kirschtorte*, the kirsch tart from Zug, or the *Rüeblitorte*, a cake made from carrots and eggs and topped with almonds, cinnamon and fruit brandy. Finally, the wonderful walnut pie is a speciality of Engadine.

Fine Swiss wine

Along with the tiny fruits that grow so well in the mountains – blueberries and raspberries, served with the rich *crème fraîche* of the Gruyère region – there are always delicious meringue desserts, served with or without whipped cream.

SWISS WINE

The reputation of Swiss wine has been steadily improving in recent years. The great wine-growing regions of Switzerland are the cantons of Valais, Vaud and Geneva. In bars and restaurants, wine can be ordered by the bottle or half-bottle, or in carafes of one or more decilitres. White wines are often remarkable here, derived mainly from the Chasselas grape, but also often from the Sylvaner (known as Johannisberg in Valais), which makes for a sweet bouquet. The best-known and most common wine is the fruity fendant, but you can also find Riesling, Pinot Gris or Pinot Blanc, Chardonnay or Dézaley, which is dry and very drinkable. Be sure to try Valais specialities such as Humagne Blanc, Petite Arvine and Amigne.

Red wines are mainly of the Gamay and Pinot Noir varieties. In Ticino, the most prevalent wine is the robust Merlot, a strong red with a lovely ruby colour. Also, try Nostrano, a heady red wine, or Mezzana, which comes in both red and

FRUIT OF THE VINE

While touring the Lake Geneva area, be sure to visit two outstanding wine regions. First is the Lavaux, situated roughly between Montreux and Lausanne. The Lavaux is not only a picturesque World Heritage Site, with steep terraces rising off the banks of the lake, but it also produces some of Switzerland's finest white wines, with notable varietals including Chasselas and Pinot Blanc. You can hike or bike along the viticulture roads while taking in views of the vineyards and the French Alps across Lake Geneva. For a tasting, give Domaine Louis Bovard in Cully a try (tel: 021 799 2125; www.domainebovard. com). The other region not to miss is located in the countryside surrounding the city of Geneva. The Route du Vignoble wine road meanders through the rolling vineyards from the charming village of Satigny to the hilly region of Dardagny close to the French border. A few producers to try: Cave Les Perrières in Peissy (tel: 022 753 9000; www.lesperrieres.ch), Domaine du Paradis in Satigny (tel: 022 753 1855; www.domaine-du-paradis.ch) and Domaine Les Hutins in Dardagny (tel: 022 754 1205; www.domaineleshutins.ch). Most wineries are open Saturday mornings for visitors.

white. The German-Swiss wines are less widely known, but some of their light dry reds (Hallauer, Maienfelder, Klevner and Stammheimer) are worth tasting.

OTHER DRINKS

Swiss blonde beers are sold under many names, both bottled and draft. Like German beers, they tend to range in strength from medium to very strong. If you don't drink alcohol, try the local fruit juices, especially apple and grape.

Fruit brandy *(eau-de-vie)* is a common after-dinner drink. Among these liquors, which are very popular in Switzerland, try apple, prune, kirsch (in Basel and Zug), the *grappa* of Ticino, the *poire William* of Valais, or *chrüter*, a herbal brandy.

COFFEE

At breakfast time, the customary drink is *Milchkaffee*, coffee with hot milk (called a *renversé* in French-speaking regions). The coffee here is generally less strong than that served in France or Italy. For an Italian-style espresso, ask for a *ristretto*. Coffee is always served with a small pot of cream; if you are lucky, the dish it comes in will be made of chocolate and filled with thick *crème fraîche*.

TO HELP YOU ORDER (...in three languages)

English French German *Italian*

Waiter/Waitress
Garçon/Mademoiselle *Garçon/Fräulein* **Cameriere**

Can we have a table, please?
Une table, s'il vous plaît. *Wir hätten gern einen Tisch.*
Possiamo avere un tavolo?

The menu, please.
La carte, s'il vous plaît. *Die Speisekarte, bitte.*
Il menu, per favore.

Do you have a special today?
Avez-vous une assiette du jour? *Haben Sie einen Tagesteller?*
  Ha il piatto del giorno?
I would like...
Je voudrais... *Ich möchte...* **Vorrei...**
a pre-dinner drink
un aperitif *einen Aperitif* **un aperitivo**

a beer une bière *einen Bier* **una birra**
butter du beurre *Butter* **del burro**
a coffee un café *einen Kaffee* **un caffè**
water de l'eau *Wasser* **dell'acqua**
cheese du fromage *Käse* **del formaggio**
milk du lait *Milch* **del latte**
bread du pain *Brot* **del pane**
fish du poisson *Fisch* **del pesce**
potatoes des pommes *Kartoffeln* **delle patate de terre**
salad de la salade *Salat* **dell'insalata**
salt du sel *Salz* **del sale**
sugar du sucre *Zucker* **dello zucchero**
tea un thé *einen Tee* **un té**
wine du vin *Wein* **del vino**

...AND READ THE MENU IN FRENCH

agneau lamb	**fraises** strawberries
asperges asparagus	**lard** bacon
bœuf beef	**macédoine de fruits**
canard duck	fruit salad
champignons mushrooms	**medallion** tender-loin
chasse game	**œufs** eggs
chevreuil venison	**pomme** apple
côte (lette) chop, cutlet	**porc** pork
entrecote steak	**poulet** chicken

raisons grapes
saucisse sausage
gigot (d'agneau) leg of lamb
glace ice-cream

jambon ham
saumon (fumé) salmon (smoked)
terrine paté
veau veal

...AND IN GERMAN

Apfel apple
Bohnen beans
Ei(er) egg(s)
Eis (Glace) ice
Ente duck
Erbsen peas
Forelle trout
Fruchsalat fruit salad
Geflügel grilled sliced vegetables
Kalbfleisch veal
Käse cheese
Kuchen cake

Lammfleisch lamb
Leber liver
Rahm cream
Reis rice
Rindfleisch beef
Rösti potatoes
Schinken ham
Schweine-fleisch pork
Spargel asparagus
Speck bacon
Teigwaren noodles
Wienerli Vienna sausage
Wurst sausage

...AND IN ITALIAN

agnello lamb
fagioli beans
fagiolini green beans
filetto filet (of beef)
formaggio cheese
fragile strawberries
frutta fruit
funghi mushrooms
gelato ice-cream
insalata salad
manzo beef

polenta polenta
pollo chicken
prosciutto ham
riso rice
spinaci spinach
trota trout
uovo(a) eggs
verdure vegetables
vitello veal
fungo mushroom
pane bread

PLACES TO EAT

We have used the following symbols to give an idea of the price for a meal for two, excluding drinks:

$$$$ over CHF100 $$ CHF50–75
$$$ CHF75–100 $ below CHF50

BASEL

Der Vierte König $$ *Blumenrain 20, tel: 061 261 5442*, http://jakob restaurants.ch/basel Overlooking the Rhine, this restaurant/ wine bar has a diverse menu with delicious soups and pastas. But wine is the focus here – evident by the bottles of wine which line the walls. The entrance is off Blumenrain as the front door faces the Rhine.

Stucki $$$$ *Bruderholzallee 42, tel: 061 361 8222*, www.stucki basel.ch. Probably Basel's most famous restaurant and one of the best in Switzerland. French cuisine that offers a changing, seasonal menu which might include Bresse chicken, Chamois or white truffles from Alba. Outdoor dining in the garden in summer. Closed Sunday and Monday.

Zum Braunen Mutz $$–$$ *Barfüsserplatz 10, tel: 061 261 3369*, www.brauner-mutz-basel.ch. Located on the busy Barfüsserplatz in the centre of Basel, Zum Braunen Mutz offers two restaurants under one roof. A casual brasserie on the ground level with outdoor terrace (great place to people watch while grabbing lunch) serving French, German and Italian specialities. More formal – and expensive – dining upstairs in the gourmet restaurant.

BERN

Altes Tramdepot $–$$ *Grosser Muristalden 6, tel: 031 368 1415*, www.altestramdepot.ch. In an old tram hall, right by the Bear Pit. This is a Brewery with typical beer-hall cuisine, such as the house speciality, Bavarian sausages with mustard and pretzel. During warmer months, there is a terrace that overlooks the city.

Kornhauskeller $$–$$$ *Kornhausplatz 18, tel: 031 327 7272*; www. kornhauskeller.ch. In an old corn cellar, this vast underground restaurant near the Kornhausbrucke was renovated to keep much of the original detail and walls of the original structure. A dark, but vibrant eatery resulted that focuses on Italian cuisine. A bistro/café above ground offers lighter fare and outdoor seating during the summer.

Wein und Sein $$$ *Münstergasse 50, tel: 031 311 9844*, www.wein undsein.ch. Located in a cellar under Bern's famous arcades. Enter through the cellar doors to this small restaurant where every night you have but one option: the menu that is designed for that day. Reservations required. Closed Sunday and Monday.

CHUR

Otello $ *Hartbertstrasse 10 tel: 081 250 55 15,* www.otello.ch. Italian restaurant that is always packed with locals and tourists. Pizza is great and there is a wide selection of wines.

DAVOS

Bistro Gentiana et Café des Artistes $$–$$$ *Promenade 53, tel: 081 413 5649*, www.gentiana.ch. In Davos-Platz, a trendy bistro with several fondue varieties and also a selection of snail dishes. Closed Wednesdays during the summer.

GENEVA

Café des Négociants $$$–$$$$ *rue de la Filature 29, tel: 022 300 3130*, www.negociants.ch. Situated just outside Geneva, but a short tram-ride away, in Carouge. One of many excellent dining options in this popular suburb. Extensive wine selection. Larger groups can eat at a big table in the wine cellar. Closed Sunday.

Demi Lune $ *rue Etienne Dumont 3, tel: 022 312 1290*, www.demilune. ch. With a swank, lounge feel, this small café is popular for a late-night cocktail or glass of wine, but also has an eclectic menu ranging from burgers and sandwiches to tapas and chicken tandoori.

L'Auberge d'Hermance $$$$ *rue du Midi 12, Hermance, tel: 022 751 1368*, www.hotel-hermance.ch. Nestling on a narrow street in the quaint village of Hermance (just before the French border along the left bank). Enchanting French restaurant with a vine-covered terrace in the summer. Closed Tuesdays and for lunch on Wednesdays. Also an inn with six rooms.

Les Armures $$–$$$ *rue du Puits-St-Pierre 1, tel: 022 310 3442*, www.hotel-les-armures.ch. Housed in the famous Hotel Les Armures in the heart of the old town. Serving some of the best fondue in Geneva as well as other traditional Swiss cuisine.

GRUYÈRES

Le Chalet $–$$ *rue du Bourg 53, tel: 026 921 2154*, www.chalet-gruyeres.ch. Great place for a quintessential, traditional Swiss dining experience from the chalet exterior to the all-wood interior to the heavy, cheese-and-meat-focused cuisine. Excellent raclette and fondue. As does much of Gruyères, caters to tourists.

GSTAAD

Chesery $$$$ *Lauenenstrasse 6, tel: 033 744 2451*, www.chesery.ch. Chef Robert Speth offers a changing menu based on the seasons. One of the finest places in the Bernese Oberland, and Switzerland. Closed Monday and usually in late spring and late autumn.

INTERLAKEN

Schuh $$ *Höheweg 56, tel: 033 888 8050*, www.schuh-interlaken.ch. Especially popular in summer because diners can sit on the large terrace, from where there are superb views of the Jungfrau. Food is decent, if not spectacular, and it's certainly eclectic, with a European, Chinese and Thai menu.

LAUSANNE

Nomade $$–$$$ *place de l'Europe 9, tel: 021 320 1313*, www.restaurantnomade.ch. A combination of *vinotheque*, bar and restaurant. The wine bar and lounge bar provide a relaxed atmosphere for grabbing a glass of wine or having a light lunch, with excellent plat du jour options. For dinner, you can dine in the more formal restaurant upstairs.

Ville de Crissier $$$$ *rue d'Yverdon 1, Crissier, tel: 021 634 0505*. According to La Liste, Ville de Crissier is the world's best restaurant for 2016. Brigitte Violier, together with new chef Franck Giovanni, continue the good work started by the late Benoît Violier. Book well in advance. Closed on Mondays.

LOCARNO

Ristorante Cittadella $$–$$$ *Via Cittadella 18, tel: 091 751 5885*, www.cittadella.ch. A trattoria downstairs and a more formal restaurant upstairs specializing in fish and seafood. Located in the Old Town. Also is a small hotel. Closed Mondays.

LUCERNE

Helvetia $–$$ *Waldstättersee 9, tel: 041 210 4450*, www.helvetia luzern.ch. No-frills decor, but the popularity of this restaurant with locals is a testimony to its home-made pasta, good variety of salads, and veal dishes as well as imaginative vegetarian dishes. There are tables outside on the square in good weather.

Old Swiss House $$$$ *Löwenplatz 4, tel: 041 410 6171*, www.old swisshouse.ch. Close to the Lion Monument, this has been a Lucerne staple for decades. The interior is decorated with antiques and is heavy on wood, befitting a Swiss chalet. Traditional cuisine. Try the house speciality, wienerschnitzel. Closed Monday.

Schiffrestaurant Wilhem Tell $$ *Landungsbrücke 9, tel. 041 410 23 30*, http://schiffrestaurant.ch A restaurant situated on a 100-year-old ship. Fondue recommended. Magnificent views of the lake. Closed on Mondays.

Taube $$ *Burgenstrasse 3, tel: 041 210 0747*, www.taube-luzern.ch. In a delightful building with a wooden bay window on the first floor, this restaurant has been feeding Lucerners since 1772. It specialises in regional dishes using seasonal ingredients.

LUGANO

Al Portone $$$ *Viale Cassarate 3, tel: 78 722 9324*, www.ristorante-alportone.ch. Close to Parco Civico, this restaurant has garnered 17 GaultMillau points to reward its creative Italian cuisine, blending traditional dishes with a modern flair. Closed Sunday and Monday and in August.

La Tinera $ *Via dei Gorini 2, tel: 091 923 5219*. In the centre of the old town, this Italian restaurant has a grotto atmosphere in its basement location. Very casual with good-value pasta dishes and other Italian specialities. Closed Sunday and Monday, and in August, and reservations are not accepted.

NEUCHÂTEL

Maison des Halles $$ *rue du Trésor 4, tel: 032 724 3141*, www.maisondeshalles.ch. A casual café with outdoor terrace, and a gourmet restaurant (for groups of 10 or more only), combine in a 16th-century building to give two fine dining options, just off the central Place des Halles.

ST-GALLEN

Jägerhof $$$$ *Brühlbleichestrasse 11, tel: 071 245 5022*, www.jaegerhof.ch. Highly awarded and stylish restaurant that uses fresh market produce to create diverse seasonal menus. Several rooms also available for accommodation.

ST MORITZ

Engiadina $–$$ *Via Dimlej 1, tel: 081 833 3000,* www.restaurant-engiadina.ch. A good place for a reasonably priced Swiss meal. The food is straightforward and hearty: fondues, carpaccio and steak. Located close to the railway station.

SCHAFFHAUSEN

Gerberstube $$$ *Bachstrasse 8, tel: 052 625 2155,* www.bindella.ch/de/gerberstube. Popular Italian restaurant serving traditional cuisine and some international specialities. Closed Sunday and Monday.

ZERMATT

Schäferstübli $$ *Riedstrasse 2, tel: 027 966 7600,* www.julen.ch. Traditional Valais and Swiss specialities are served, including fondues and raclette. The family-run hotel Julen also has a more upscale restaurant with an international menu.

ZURICH

Hiltl $ *Sihlstrasse 28, tel: 044 227 7000,* www.hiltl.ch. The oldest vegetarian restaurant in Europe, Hiltl has been a Zurich landmark for more than 100 years. The menu encompasses a multitude of different salads, pastas, curries and fruit juices, among other choices. On tram lines 2 and 9.

Kronenhalle $$$–$$$$ *Rämistrasse 4, tel: 044 262 9900,* www.kronenhalle.com. One of Zurich's most popular restaurants. Serves excellent French international cuisine in a traditional French brasserie atmosphere. Close to Bellevue tram stop on lines 2, 4, 8, 9 and 11.

Rosaly's $$ *Freieckgasse 7, tel: 044 261 4430,* www.rosalys.ch. A popular bar and restaurant that combines produce of the season with a Californian flair. Diverse soups and salads are offered here, along with some creative daily specials. Live music some Saturdays.

A-Z TRAVEL TIPS

A Summary of Practical Information

A

ACCOMMODATION (see also Camping and Youth Hostels)

Hotels of all categories are listed on the Swiss Hotel Association website (www.swisshotels.com) which lists hotels by category, region, hotel group and character – for example, hotels for gourmets or spa facilities. Information concerning families, senior citizens and facilities for the disabled can be found at Swiss National Tourist Offices abroad and at many travel agencies.

Tourist offices can tell you what type of accommodation is available (hotels of every category, pensions with full or partial board and apartment-hotels that offer a choice of rooms, studios or apartments).

Private rooms. Tourist offices will provide a list of rooms for rent in private homes – the Swiss equivalent of bed-and-breakfast. You can also knock on the door of houses that advertise a room to rent (chambre à louer/Zimmer zu vermieten/camere da affitare) outside.

Chalets and apartments. To rent a chalet or apartment, ask a travel agent at home or in Switzerland, check with the tourist information office (they have brochures for popular regions), or look in classified ads or on the Internet. Two good sites are Interhome www.interhome.ch and My Switzerland www.my switzerland.com.

I would like a single/double room with bath/shower.
J'aimerais une chambre à un lit/deux lits/ avec bains/ douche. *Ich möchte ein Einzelzimmer/ Doppelzimmer* mit Bad/Dusche.**Vorrei una camera singolo/doppia con bagno/doccia**.
What is the rate per night?
Quel est le prix pour une nuit? *Was kostet eine Übernachtung?* **Quanto costa per notte?**

AIRPORTS *(aéroport/Flughafen/aeroporto)*

Switzerland's three major international airports are, in order of importance: **Zurich-Kloten**, **Geneva-Cointrin** and **Basel/Mulhouse**. Swiss (formerly Swissair), the national carrier, provides frequent flights to these airports. Internal flights are limited; most people take the train. The airports of Bern and Lugano are smaller, but still offer some direct flights to other countries.

A train service makes the 10-minute trip from Zurich-Kloten airport to the city's main railway station four or five times an hour and every 10 minutes in peak periods. From Geneva-Cointrin, there are six departures an hour during peak time to the Gare Cornavin, the main railway station in the centre of Geneva, a six-minute trip, continuing to many other destinations. The airports at Bern and Lugano provide shuttle bus connections to their appropriate city centres, with departures every half-hour (there are pickups at each airline). A bus connects Basel airport with the city centre several times an hour during peak hours and at least twice an hour at other times.

Fly-Rail baggage service. If you're departing from Zurich or Geneva on a scheduled or charter flight, you can register baggage all the way to your final destination at many Swiss railway stations (www.sbb.cg). Some large railway stations (over 50) also have a check-in station and will issue you an airline boarding card (this is included in the price of sending your bags). The fee is well worth it. This service is also available upon arrival in Switzerland.

B

BICYCLE RENTAL

You can hire a range of bikes *(bicyclette/Velo/bicicletta)*, including E-bikes and children's bikes at any major railway station (about 80 across the country) and return it (for a fee of CHF10) to any station that accepts bikes (check before) during opening hours at the baggage counter. Pick up leaflets describing biking paths at tourist information offices.

BUDGETING FOR YOUR TRIP

Switzerland has a reputation as an expensive country. Given the strength of its currency and the extensive development of its tourism industry, prices are generally comparable to those in major tourist destinations elsewhere in Europe. Prices are higher in fashionable resorts and in big cities such as Geneva and Zurich, but vary relatively little between regions. Below are some average prices in Swiss francs (CHF).

Bus. CHF2.60 for a short trip; day passes CHF5–10.

Bicycle hire. CHF30–35 (24 hours).

Ski equipment hire. Cross-country CHF50+ per day, CHF190+ per week. Downhill skiing, CHF60+ per day, CHF230+ per week. Prebooking online can often save you over 20 percent.

Meals and drinks. Breakfast CHF12, lunch (in a good restaurant) CHF25–40, daily special CHF20–30, dinner CHF45–60, fondue CHF20–30, coffee CHF3.50, draft beer (1/2 litre) CHF5, bottle of wine (1/2 litre) CHF20–30, non-alcoholic drinks CHF5.

Swiss Pass (second class, includes most mountain railways and lake steamers). CHF 210 (3 days), CHF251 (4 days), CHF363 (8 days), CHF440 (15 days).

C

CAMPING

Several hundred campsites, some in the Alps, are approved by the Swiss Camping and Caravan Association (tel: 031 852 0626, www.swisscamps.ch). Ask for the Swiss camping guide at a local Swiss tourist office (see page 178), at the Swiss Touring Club, Camping Division, Chemin de Blandonnet 4, 1214 Vernier (tel: 0844 888 111, www.tcs.ch), or at bookshops.

CAR HIRE

To hire a car you must produce a valid driving licence, held for a minimum of one year. You must be at least 25 years old. You can hire a car at many railway stations. Agencies usually waive cash deposits for clients with recognised credit cards.

CLIMATE

In general, Switzerland's climate is continental. The winters are cold and snowy (especially in the mountains); the summers are hot with occasional storms. Spring tends to be cool and unpredictable, autumn usually stable and mild. All year, temperatures can vary considerably within a few hours, a few kilometres or a few hundred metres of altitude. It may be pouring rain in northern Switzerland and perfectly sunny in Ticino or Engadine. The chart shows the average daytime temperature in Geneva, month by month:

	J	F	M	A	M	J	J	A	S	O	N	D
°C	0	1	5	9	13	17	18	18	14	9	4	1
°F	32	34	41	48	55	63	65	65	57	48	39	34

CLOTHING

In view of the unpredictable weather patterns, it is best to be prepared for anything. In the summer, don't forget to take along a raincoat and umbrella, as well as a jacket or sweater. In winter, bring a warm coat and lined, waterproof snow boots for the mountains.

CRIME AND SAFETY (see also Emergencies)

Muggings and violent crimes are rare in Switzerland, where you can generally come and go, day and night, in peace. Nevertheless it is always wise to lock your car and put your valuables in the hotel safe. During the winter, keep your skis in a safe place: they can easily disappear from car roof-racks and from outside après-ski spots.

D

DISABLED TRAVELLERS

The country is well adapted for disabled travellers, though difficulties can arise with public transport on secondary routes and mountain railways where platforms are commonly at a low level. However, ramps to raise wheelchairs to carriage floor level are provided at many stations. Swiss Federal Railways offers a service geared to customers with reduced mobility. Up to one hour before train departure, a free call to 0800 007 102 will produce help with boarding and alighting from trains in one of the 170 staffed stations. Switzerland Tourism offices can also provide advice and lists of hotels with disabled access.

DRIVING (see also Car Hire)

To bring your car into Switzerland, you'll need a national driving licence, car registration papers and your Green Card (a recommended but not obligatory extension to your regular car insurance policy, validating it for foreign countries). A nationality code sticker must be visible at the rear of your car, and you must have a red warning triangle reflector for use in case of a breakdown. Seat belts are obligatory both in town and in the country. In winter you may be required to use snow chains on Alpine passes. These can be obtained at petrol stations along the way.

On the road. Drive on the right and give priority to the right unless otherwise indicated. On mountain roads, leave the awesome views to the passengers; to admire the scenery in safety, stop at roadside parking areas. On difficult stretches of mountain roads, right-of-way is given to postal buses or otherwise to the ascending vehicle. Honking your horn is recommended on blind corners of mountain roads; avoid it everywhere else. In general roads are good, and there is a well-developed motorway network linking all the big towns.

Autoroute tax. An annual road tax of CHF40 is levied on all cars and motorcycles using Swiss autoroutes. An additional fee of

CHF40 applies to trailers and caravans. The *vignette* (sticker) is valid from 1 December of the year preceding the date stamped on the vignette to 31 January of the following year. It can be purchased from customs officers at border crossings or at any post office and is valid for multiple re-entry into Switzerland throughout its period of validity.

Speed limits. On the green signposted highways *(autoroute/ Autobahn/autostrada)*, the maximum speed is 120kph (75mph). On other roads the limit is 80kph (50mph) unless otherwise indicated. In residential areas the speed limit is generally restricted to 50kph (31mph), although you might encounter sections posted at either 60kph (37mph) or 30kph (19mph). Cars towing caravans and trailers may not exceed 80kph (50mph), even on highways.

Car trouble. If your car breaks down, call the tcs or Swiss Touring Club *(Touring Club Suisse/Touring-Club Schweiz/Touring Club Svizzero*, tel: 0800 140 140). It is also a good idea to contact an international insurance company before leaving to cover costs, otherwise, you will be responsible for the full price of paying a mechanic or tow truck. You can get help at any public telephone by dialling 140. Emergency telephones are installed at regular intervals along motorways.

Parking. Try to avoid parking in congested central shopping zones or historic city centres. Most cities have adopted a system of parking meters or blue zones *(zone bleu/Blaue Zona/zona blu)* and red zones *(zone rouge/Rote Zone/zona rossa)*, which limit parking time to, respectively, 1½ hours and 15 hours. To park in these zones, marked with blue or red paint, you must display a parking disc *(disc de stationnement, Parkscheibe/disco orario)* on the dashboard indicating when you left your car (some blue zones require a paid parking sticker). The parking discs are given out free of charge at petrol stations, banks and police stations. Paid carparks are also widely available. Rarely seen 'white zones' allow for unlimited parking.

Road signs. Most signs in Switzerland conform to international norms. Here are the translations for some common signs:

exit sortie *Ausfahrt* **uscita**
airport aéroport *Flughafen* **aeroporto**
icy road verglas *Glatteis* **strada ghiacitta**
city centre centre-ville *Stadtzentrum* **centro città**
detour deviation *Umleitung* **deviazione**
customs douane *Zoll* **dogana**

E

ELECTRICITY

The standard electric current is 220 V, 50 Hz. Most appliances set for 240 V will operate on 220 V, but alter the setting if possible.

EMBASSIES AND CONSULATES *(Ambassade, Consulat/ Botschaft, Konsulate/Ambasciata, Consolato)*

All embassies, located in Bern, have their own consular sections. Some countries also have consulates in Geneva, Zurich and other cities.

Australia: Consulate General: Chemin des Fins 2, PO Box 172, 1211 Geneva 19, tel: 022 799 9100, www.australia.ch.

Canada: Kirchenfeldstrasse 88, 3000 Bern 6, tel: 031 357 3200, www.canadainternational.gc.ca.

Ireland: Kirchenfeldstrasse 68, PO Box 262, 3005 Bern, tel: 031 352 1442, www.embassyofireland.ch.

New Zealand: Mission and Consulate General: Chemin des Fins 2, Grand-Saconnex 1218 Geneva, tel: 022 929 0350, www.mfat.govt.nz.

South Africa: Alpenstrasse 29, 3006 Bern, tel: 031 350 1313, www. southafrica.ch.

UK: Thunstrasse 50, 3005 Bern, tel: 031 359 7700, https://www.gov. uk/government/world/organisations/british-embassy-berne. Vice-Consulate: Hegibachstrasse 47, 8032 Zurich, tel: 044 383 6560.

US: Sulgeneckstrasse 19, CH-3007 Bern, tel: 031 357 7011, 031 357

7234, http://bern.usembassy.gov.
Geneva consulate: Rue François Versonnex 7, 1207 Geneva, tel: 022 840 5160.
Zurich consulate: Dufourstrasse 101, 8008 Zurich, tel: 043 499 2960.

EMERGENCIES *(urgences/Notfall /emergenza)*
Police **117**
Fire **118**
Roadside assistance **140**
Paramedics, ambulance **144**

For a chemist, doctor or dentist on 24-hour duty, consult the daily local paper. The addresses of chemists open on Sundays and holidays are posted in the window of other branches.

G

GAY AND LESBIAN TRAVELLERS
Most cities and large towns have lively gay communities. A good source of information is the Switzerland Tourism website (www.my switzerland.com), which covers bars, clubs, restaurants and events. For Zurich, try the city's gay websites (www.zuerigay.ch and http://zurich.gaycities.com).

GETTING THERE
By air. From Great Britain and Ireland. There are frequent daily flights from London to Basel, Zurich and Geneva, several to Bern and two a day to Lugano via Bern. You can also fly to Zurich from Edinburgh, Manchester and Birmingham. You can also fly to Zurich from Belfast, Birmingham, Bournemouth, Bristol, Cardiff, East Midlands, Edinburgh, Exeter, Glasgow, Leeds Bradford, Liverpool, Manchester, Newcastle and Southampton. There are one or two flights a day from Dublin to Zurich and several a week to Geneva.

From North America. There are several direct flights a day from

New York to Zurich and Geneva, and a few to Basel with connections. There is at least one flight a day from Montreal and Toronto to Zurich.

From the southern hemisphere. From Australia and New Zealand you can catch daily flights to Switzerland with one change. There is at least one flight a day from South Africa.

Internal flights. Internal flights are limited thanks to excellent rail links from Geneva and Zurich airports to many other destinations, and due to the small size of the country. Darwin Airline (www. etihadregional.com) runs many of the connections.

Discounts and special fares. Offers vary from one travel agent or airline to another. It is best to enquire directly about special fares. Swiss consulates abroad can guide you to agencies specialising in travel to Switzerland.

Package trips. There are many options for fixed-price travel. Packages may include your flight, hotel or apartment and car hire, *à la carte* trips, trips with train fares and hotel included, driving trips and 'theme' trips (art, sports, etc.). Ask your travel agent for details.

By rail. The journey from London to Paris aboard the Eurostar high-speed train (TGV or *train à grande vitesse*, tel: 08705 186 186, www.eurostar.com) takes 2 hours 20 minutes via the Channel Tunnel. After a change of stations in Paris, you can reach Geneva (3 hours 5 minutes), Bern and Basel (3 hours 30 minutes), Lausanne (4 hours) and Zurich (4 hours 50 minutes) by direct TGV.

From Paris. There are five or six TGVs a day to Geneva and four or five to Lausanne. There is one direct TGV a day from Paris to Bern, or you can take one of several daily trains and change in Basel or Geneva. There are four direct TGVs a day from Paris to Zurich. There are also several trains between Paris and Evian. Paris to Basel trains leave four times a day, and there is a direct train between Nice and Geneva.

From Spain. There are trains from Barcelona to Geneva, including a night train (Trainhotel), which goes on to Lausanne and Zurich.

By road. The itineraries noted here, usually on highways, are the fastest and most comfortable routes. Travel time corresponds to the average trip taken in normal traffic conditions. Also contact your country's Touring Club before travelling for detailed information.

Book your passage on **car ferries** well in advance. Fares are cheaper for midweek sailings, and the price fluctuates seasonally. The best route is Calais–Reims–Chaumont–Basel–Zurich or Calais/Bologne–Paris–Geneva.

There are regular **coach** services between London's Victoria Station and Basel, Geneva, Wurzburg and Zurich. These trips take roughly 18 hours (go to www.nationalexpress.com for information).

From Belgium. From Brussels to Geneva via Sterpenich (A6), Bourg-en-Bresse (A39) and St-Julien (A40/A401) is 812km/508 miles (8 hours 50 minutes). Between Brussels and Zurich via Luxembourg, Sterpenich (A6), Strasbourg (A4) and Basel–St-Louis is a total of 665km/415 miles (7 hours 40 minutes).

From France. Paris and Geneva are 535km/335 miles (6 hours 10 minutes) apart via Beaune-Nord (A6/A31) and St-Julien (A40-A401). From Paris to Lausanne is a trip of 535km/335 miles (6 hours 20 minutes) via Beaune-Nord (A6/A31) and Vallorbe (A9). Paris/Zurich is a distance of 650km/406 miles via Beaune-Nord (A6/A31), Belfort (A36) and Mulhouse/Basel–St-Louis (A2). Nice/Geneva: 545km/340 miles (6 hours 40 minutes) via Menton/Grimaldi (A8/A10), Turin (A5), Aosta, Annemasse (A40) and Thonex. From Nice, Digne and Sisteron, you can also reach Geneva by the Napoleon highway (Gap) or the Alpen route (Croix-Haute pass) in Grenoble; take the A41 highway to the border of Switzerland.

GUIDES AND TOURS

Multilingual guides are available through the tourist offices in most cities and towns, and most offer walking tours taking in the principal attractions, though most will be in German or French. The main cities offer excursions, though the excellent public transport system effectively reduces demand for day itineraries, especially when so many visitors travel on a form of Swiss Travel System pass (see page 178).

H

HEALTH AND MEDICAL CARE

Most major tourist resorts have clinics, and all cities are served by modern, well-equipped hospitals. The standard of treatment is high. For less serious ailments, a chemist *(pharmacie/Apotheke/farmacia)* will dispense medication and suggest a doctor if necessary.

EU citizens should get a European Health Insurance Card (EHIC) before departing, available from post offices or online, entitling them to reduced-cost, or free, medical treatment. To cover all eventualities a travel insurance policy is advisable, and for non-EU residents, essential.

> **I need a doctor/a dentist.**
> Il me faut un médecin/un dentiste. *Ich brauche einen Arzt/einen Zahnarzt.* **Ho bisogno di un medico/un dentista.**

L

LANGUAGE

Switzerland has four national languages: German, French, Italian and Romansh. Swiss German or Schwyzerdütsch, spoken by nearly two-thirds of the population (in the country's north and centre), groups a number of dialects which are often incomprehensible to a speaker of High German. Hochdeutsch or literary German, which German-speaking Swiss learn at school, is like a foreign tongue to them.

Italian is spoken only in Ticino (in the south) and parts of Grisons. Scwyzerdütsch and Romansh are also spoken in parts of these regions. Romansh comes from low Latin and has several dialects. French is spoken mainly in the west of the country but is understood everywhere.

The Swiss tend to be good at learning foreign languages and often speak two, three or even four languages. Many people speak English well enough to help you find your way around.

When you enter an office or shop, remember the Swiss German expression *Grüzi (mitenand)*, which means roughly 'Good morning (everyone)'. In Italian, you can say *buon giorno* (good morning) or *buona sera* ('good evening'). When you leave, say *adieu (mitenand)* or *arrivederci* if you are in Ticino. In response, you may hear *Uf wiederluege* ('until next time') or *a presto* ('until soon').

Do you speak English?
Parlez-vous anglais? *Sprechen Sie Englisch?* **Parla inglese?**
Help me, please.
Aidez-moi, s'il vous plaît. *Helfen Sie mir, bitte.* **Mi aiuti, per favore.**
I don't understand.
Je ne comprends pas. *Ich verstehe nicht.* **Non capisco.**
yes/no oui/non *ja/nein* **si/no**
please s'il vous plaît *bitte* **per favore**
thank you merci *danke* **grazie**
when/where quand/où *wann/wo* **quando/dove**
how comment *wie* **come**
good/bad bon/mauvais *gut/schlecht* **buono/cattivo**
big/small grand/petit *gross/klein* **grande/piccolo**
cold/hot froid/chaud *kalt/heiss* **freddo/caldo**
open/closed ouvert/fermé *offen/geschlossen* **aperto/chiuso**

M

MAPS

Bookshops, stationery shops and some newspaper stands offer a wide selection of road and regional maps, as well as city maps.

Tourist offices, car-hire agencies and the larger banks distribute excellent city maps.

Hikers will find indispensable topographical maps at local or regional tourist offices. Switzerland's well-maintained footpaths are also well-marked with yellow blazes and signposts that display the average time for a given hike. Good walking maps are published by Kümmerly + Frey and the Federal Office of Topography.

MEDIA

Newspapers. Even in small towns, newsstands stock a surprisingly wide variety of foreign papers, plus all the Swiss newspapers. The best selection and earliest delivery are offered by main railway stations and airports. English-language daily newspapers such as the *International Herald Tribune*, *USA Today*, *Wall Street Journal Europe* and *European Financial Times* are available on the day of publication.

Magazines and books. There are several monthly magazines published in Switzerland, including *Swiss News* and *Earth Focus*. English-language magazines of all kinds are widely available across the country. In most large towns you will find English-language bookshops. Any serious bookshop will offer at least a small selection of English-language paperbacks.

Television and radio. There are four Swiss cable TV stations (in French, German and Italian, which can be tuned in without cable as well), plus German, Austrian and Italian stations. Some of the programmes are dual-language broadcasts, showing films in French, German or Italian and the original language, very often English. English-language cable TV stations include CNBC Europe, CNN International, Eurosport, MTV Europe and BBC World. Cable radio stations usually include BBC World Service and BBC Foreign Language Service, Sky Radio, Voice of America and Swiss Radio International English Service (online service at www.swissinfo.org) plus a number of FM stations from Switzerland (both local, like

World Radio in Geneva, and national). Depending where you are, you might pick up stations from Germany, Austria, France or Italy.

MONEY

Currency. The monetary unit of Switzerland is the Swiss franc *(franc suisse/Schweizer Franken/franco svizzero)*, which is usually abbreviated as CHF or SFr. It is divided into 100 centimes *(Rappen/centesini)*, abbreviated Rp. in German and ct. in French or Italian. **Coins:** 5, 10, 20 and 50 centimes; 1, 2 and 5 francs (the latter is often called *cent sous*). **Notes:** 10, 20, 50, 100, 200 and 1,000 francs.

Banks. Most banks are open weekdays 8.30am–12.30pm and 1.30–4.30, 5 or 5.30pm. Main branches generally remain open during lunch hour. One day a week, branches stay open until 6 or 6.30pm. Currency exchange offices at airports and the larger railway stations do business from around 6.30am–7.30pm every day. There is no charge to change Swiss or foreign money, buy or sell traveller's cheques in different currencies or cash Eurocheques. Cashpoints (atm machines) can be found nearly everywhere and accept cards in the Eu network.

Credit cards. Smaller businesses, particularly in remote regions or small villages, may not accept credit cards, but they are widely accepted in major establishments and in large cities.

Traveller's cheques. The well-known international cheques are generally accepted everywhere. The exchange rate for traveller's cheques is better in banks than elsewhere. You must show your passport when cashing a traveller's cheque.

O

OPENING HOURS (see also Public Holidays)

Most offices are open 8am–noon and 1.30 or 2–5pm (sometimes 6pm), Monday to Friday.

Department stores and most other shops open at 8am (some

at 8.30 or 9am) until 6.30 or 7pm. Some neighbourhood or village grocery stores open at 7am and close for lunch, as do most boutiques, except in the larger cities. In some cities, closing time is extended until 9pm one night a week. Some businesses close for a half-day during the week – often Monday morning or Wednesday, Thursday or Saturday afternoon. On Saturdays, many shops open 8am–4, 5 or 5.30pm, depending on the region. On Sundays, everything closes except for a few food stores (which stay open all or part of the day). In ski resorts during the high season, boutiques are open all week.

Museum hours vary, but in general they are open to the public from Tuesday to Sunday 10am–noon and 2–5 or 6pm. Large museums and museums in big cities generally stay open through lunch.

P

POLICE *(police/Polizei/polizia)*

Switzerland does not have a uniformed federal police. Law and order is the responsibility of the individual cantons and communities, so police uniforms vary greatly from one place to the next. Police are armed, efficient and courteous. Law enforcement is strict.

The emergency telephone number for the police is **117**.

Where is the nearest police station?
Où est le poste de police le plus proche? *Wo ist die nächste Polizeiwache?* **Dove si trova il posto di polizia più vicino?**

POST OFFICES *(bureau de poste/ Post/ufficio postale)*

In addition to normal postal business, post offices handle telegrams and bill-paying. They are generally open from 7.30am until noon and from 1.30pm until 6 or 6.30pm, depending on the size of the office, and from 7.30 to 11am on Saturdays. In big cities, major post office stays open at lunchtime, and a window reserved for urgent mail stays open until 10pm, sometimes later. In smaller towns, hours may vary.

You can also buy stamps at machines outside the post office or at the railway station, newsstands, tobacco shops, souvenir shops (since they sell postcards) or at the hotel. Swiss mailboxes are yellow.

If you don't know in advance where you will be staying in Switzerland, you can have your mail addressed to the general delivery desk (poste restante/postlagernd/fermo posta) at the main post office of any town you expect to visit.

express mail par exprès *Express* **espresso**
registered en recommandé *eingeschrieben* **raccomandata**
a stamp un timbre *eine Briefmarke* **un francobollo**

PUBLIC HOLIDAYS (jours fériés/gesetzliche Feiertage/feste)

The holiday calendar varies from one canton to the next, according to the local history and religious traditions. Here are the official Swiss holidays, observed all over the country unless noted otherwise:

New Year (1 Jan) Nouvel An *Neujahr* **Capodanno**
Good Friday Vendredi-Saint *Karfreitag* **Venerdi Santo**
Easter Monday* Lundi de Páques *Ostermonta*g **Lunedì di Pasqua**
Ascension Day Ascension *Auffahrt* **Ascensione**
Monday of Pentecost* Lundi de Pentecôte *Pfingstmontag* **Lunedi di Pentecoste**
Swiss National Day (1 Aug) Fête national *Bundesfeier* **Festa nazionale**
Christmas (25 Dec) Noël *Weihnachten* **Natale**
St Stephen's Day* (26 Dec) Saint-Etienne *Stefanstag* **Santo Stefano**
*Holidays celebrated in nearly all cantons

On these holidays, banks and stores stay closed all day; the same is true for 1 May in certain cantons. Catholic cantons also observe the day of the Immaculate Conception (8 December).

PUBLIC TRANSPORT

Train (see page 159). Both the Swiss Federal Railways (CFF/SBB/FFS; www.sbb.ch) and smaller private railways live up to the Swiss reputation: fast, clean and punctual, although heavy snowfalls may cause delays. Trains run at regular intervals, with at least an hourly service generally provided between all major cities and even smaller towns. Intercity trains are air-conditioned, with first- and second-class cars. In addition some offer 'family cars', equipped with game rooms where children can play during the trip, and 'quiet cars'. Direct trains *(train direct/Schnellzug/treno diretto)* are express trains serving major cities and medium-sized towns. Regional trains *(train régional/Regionalzug/treno regionale)* are local trains making all station stops.

Timetables are posted in every station, and listed connecting trains are always guaranteed. Tickets can be bought from ticket windows or automatic machines and will be punched on the train by an inspector.

There are several systems of passes good for train travel throughout Switzerland: The **Eurailpass** in all its categories (Eurail Youthpass, Eurail Saverpass, Eurail Flexipass, Eurail Flexipass Youth and Eurail Saver Flexipass) is available only to non-European residents. It is issued in the holder's home country (www.raileurope.com).

The **Inter Rail** pass comes in four categories according to age (adults, under 26 and children ages 4–11). The EuroDomino pass offers between 3 and 8 days of unlimited travel in a specified country out of a choice of 28. These are available at all railway stations, many travel agencies or online at www.raileurope.co.uk.

For most visitors, the best option is the ranges of passes covering the **Swiss Travel System** (STS) since they cover most forms of public transport throughout the country. These practical and economical tickets are available to anyone living outside Switzerland.

The **Swiss Pass** allows unrestricted rail, postal bus or boat travel for periods of 3, 4, 8, or 15 days. Trams and buses in many cities are also included, as are discounts of 25–50 percent on those mountain trains and panoramic routes not covered by the passes. The **Swiss Youth Pass** (under 26) gives a 25 percent discount on the price of the Swiss Pass. The **Swiss Flexipass** is valid for travel on any three, five or six days within one month and includes the same reductions that are available with the Swiss Pass. The **Swiss Card** offers you one month of half-price travel by train, postal bus or boat (including a special discount of 25–50 percent on most mountain trains), in addition to free round-trip connections between the airport or border train station and the town you are travelling to). With the **Family Pass**, children under 16 accompany their parents free.

Apply for the passes at travel agencies or Swiss tourist offices abroad (though the Swiss Card is available only at airport and border stations in Switzerland). You can also get STS passes in any of Switzerland's major railway stations, (bring your passport). For more details contact Swiss Federal Railways SBB, Hochschulstrasse 6, CH3000 Bern 65, tel: +41 (0)900 300 300, www.sbb.ch; or the SBB Travel Bureau at Zurich or Geneva airports; or visit https://traintickets.myswitzerland.com, which also provides information on many Swiss scenic trains.

Postal bus. Wherever the trains don't go, the bright yellow postal buses do. They carry mail and passengers over mountain roads to the smallest of hamlets. Their trustworthy drivers have been trained to manoeuvre on the most fearsome mountain roads in any weather.

Connections between trains and postal buses are scheduled for convenience. You can buy tickets at the train station, on the bus or sometimes at the post office (tel: 0848 888 888, www.postbus.ch).

Boat. Switzerland's great lakes are all crisscrossed by sizeable passenger boats, often with paddle-wheels. Many have their own restaurants. From Lausanne, the Lake of Geneva (*Lac Léman*) ferries are the fastest way to get to France (frequent departures every day for

Evian). There are also daily tours around the lake from June to September. Every Sunday in winter, a boat makes the round-trip journey from Lausanne to Vevey, Montreux, Villeneuve and St-Gingolphe.

Bus or tram. All Swiss cities have efficient public transport networks (bus, trolley-bus or tram). Tickets are available from machines at each stop. You can sometimes buy them on board, although that will usually be more expensive. Be sure to hold on to your ticket, as they are frequently checked by roving conductors. You can also buy books of 10 tickets or 24-hour passes *(carte de 24 heures/Tageskarte/abbonamento giornaliero)*; ask at major bus stops or newsstands.

Taxi. You can always hail a passing taxi, but on rainy days, it might be a better bet to head directly to a cab stand (on major squares or around railway stations) or to reserve by phone. Though fares vary from city to city, they are always high. All taxis have a meter and a table listing additional charges for extras such as baggage. Tips are generally included in the price (see Tipping).

first/second class
première/seconde classe erste/zweite Klasse **prima/seconda classe**
one-way/return (round trip)
aller simple/aller-retour einfach/retour **andata/andata e ritorno**
Where is the nearest bus stop?
Où est l'arrêt de bus le plus proche? Wo ist die nächste Bushaltestelle? **Dovè si trova la fermata d'auto bus più vicina?**

T

TELEPHONES *(téléphone/Telefon/telefono)*
Public phone booths can be used for direct international calls. To

use the majority of public phones you will need a *Taxcard*, a magnetic calling card available at post offices and newsstands. You can also use Visa, Eurocard or American Express.

TIME ZONE
Switzerland is on Central European Time, which is Greenwich Mean Time +1 hour. In summer, Daylight Savings Time is applied at the same dates as in neighbouring countries.

TIPPING *(pourboire/Trinkgeld /mancia)*
Tips are generally included in the bill, but for exceptional service, you may round off the total or leave an extra 5 percent. Porters will expect a coin. Taxi drivers also get a tip, usually around 10 percent.

TOILETS
Public toilets are clean and easily accessible, sometimes with a small charge. They are marked *Mesdames* (in French), *Damen/Frauen* (in Swiss German) or *signore/donne* (in Ticino) for women, and *Messieurs*, *Herren/Männer* or *signori/uomini*, for men.

TOURIST INFORMATION
In major cities throughout the world, you will find a Swiss National Tourist Office to assist with the planning of your trip.

UK and Ireland: Switzerland Tourism, Swiss Centre, 30 Bedford Street, London WC2E 9ED, tel: 00800 100 200 29, email: info.uk@myswitzerland.com.

US: Switzerland Tourism, 608 Fifth Avenue, New York, NY 10020, tel: 1-800-794-7795 or 011800-100-200-30, email: info.usa@myswitzerland.com.

Canada: Switzerland Tourism, 48 University Avenue, Suite 1500, CA-Toronto, Ontario M5G 1V2, tel: 1-800-794 7795 (toll free), email: info.caen@myswitzerland.com.

In Switzerland itself, the head branch of the Swiss National Tourist Office is located at Tödistrasse 7, CH-8027 Zurich, tel: 044 288 1111 or 008 00100 20029, www.myswitzerland.com. This website has a great deal of information on the many different regions in Switzerland.

Every region, city and resort has its own tourist office *(office de tourisme/Verkehrsburo* or *Verkehrsverein/ente per il turismo)*, with free brochures, lists of hotels and maps. Each has its own website with details of its location.

V

VISAS AND ENTRY REQUIREMENTS

Most visitors – including citizens of the UK, the US, Canada and most other English-speaking countries – need only a valid passport to enter Switzerland. You are entitled to stay for up to 90 days without further formality. In 2005, Switzerland approved the Schengen Agreement, easing the flow of travel between other Schengen countries in Europe with a special visa. Check with the Swiss embassy in your own country for information on obtaining this visa.

You may take the following duty-free into Switzerland: 200 cigarettes or 50 cigars or 250g tobacco (European visitors), or 400 cigarettes or 100 cigars or 500g tobacco (non-European visitors), plus 1 litre spirits and 2 litres wine (either).

When returning to your own country you may take: **Australia:** 250 cigarettes or 250g of cigars or 250g tobacco, plus 2.25 litres of spirits and wine in total; **Canada:** 200 cigarettes and 50 cigars and 200g tobacco, plus 1.1 litres spirits or 1.5 litres wine; **Ireland:** 800 cigarettes or 200 cigars or 1kg tobacco, plus 10 litre spirits or 90 litres wine; **New Zealand:** 200 cigarettes or 50 cigars or 250g tobacco, plus 1.125 litres spirits or 4.5 litres wine; **South Africa:** 200 cigarettes or 20 cigars or 250g tobacco, plus 1 litre spirits and

1 litre wine; **UK:** 200 cigarettes or 50 cigars or 250g tobacco, plus 1 litre spirits and 2 litres wine; **US:** 200 cigarettes and 100 cigars (no Cuban cigars) and a reasonable quantity of tobacco, plus 1 litre spirits or 1 litre wine.

Monetary restrictions. There is no restriction on the import or export of either Swiss or foreign currencies.

W

WEBSITES AND INTERNET ACCESS

www.myswitzerland.com Swiss tourism.

www.swissinfo.ch, www.swissworld.org General information and news.

www.swisshotels.ch Booking site for hotels and inns.

www.romantikhotels.ch, www.relaischateaux.com Hotel group sites with several unique hotels and inns in Switzerland.

www.gstaad.ch, www.interlaken.ch, www.stmoritz.ch, www.verbier. ch, www.zermatt.ch Regional resort sites with information on accommodation and snow reports.

Internet access can be found in many cafes and bars, though be prepared to pay. Paradoxically the more expensive hotels often tend to charge for internet access, whereas many cheaper hotels offer it free.

Y

YOUTH HOSTELS *(auberge de jeunesse/Jugendherberge/ostello della gioventù)*

There is no age limit for youth hostels, but those under 25 have priority. Reservations are recommended during the high season. For a complete list of hostels and their rules, write to: Swiss Youth Hostels, Schaffhauserstrasse 14, CH-8042 Zurich, tel: 044 360 1414, www.youthhostel.ch.

RECOMMENDED HOTELS

The following hotels in cities and resorts throughout Switzerland are listed alphabetically. Consider making reservations well in advance, particularly in the winter resorts from late December through till March. Many hotels in resort towns will require a seven-night minimum stay during the high season.

Prices normally include all taxes, but some will have an extra service charge or city tax. Breakfast is often included. Low-season rates can be much lower and, in many of the big cities, there are often reduced weekend rates. Also note, all Basel hotels come with a mobility ticket providing free public transport during your visit. These symbols represent an approximate guide in Swiss Francs for a double room with bath or shower during the high season.

$$$$$	over CHF450
$$$$	CHF300–450
$$$	CHF200–300
$$	CHF150–200
$	below CHF150

APPENZELL

Romantik Hotel Säntis $$–$$$ *Landsgemeindeplatz, tel: 071 788 1111*, www.saentis-appenzell.ch. This small, family-run hotel with a beautiful façade enjoys a prominent location on Appenzell's main square. Modern rooms, but some can be noisy if facing the Platz. The hotel's restaurant offers excellent regional cuisine and good wine at reasonable prices. 36 rooms.

BASEL

Der Teufelhof Basel $$$–$$$$ *Leonhardsgraben 47–49, tel: 061 261 1010*, www.teufelhof.com. Art and theatre are the focus here as two small hotels are combined with a small theatre. The Art Hotel has eight rooms and a suite, each individually designed. The Gallery Hotel consists of 24 rooms in a former convent where artists exhibit their work.

The small theatre is usually open during the winter months. There are two restaurants and a gourmet food and wine cellar. In the old town.

Hotel Basel $$$-$$$$ *Münzgasse 12, tel: 061 264 6800*, www.hotel-basel.ch. A well-maintained, business-orientated hotel with an efficient and courteous staff, located in the heart of the old town. Modern, spacious rooms, and a variety of suites also available. 72 rooms.

Hotel Brasserie Au Violon $-$$ *Im Lohnhof 4, tel: 061 269 8711*, www.au-violon.com. For a unique experience, stay at this former prison in a quiet courtyard just above the old town. Renovated to keep a Spartan feel, the rooms are a bit small with low doorways, but clean. You can also stay in the former police station with views over the city. Popular French brasserie by the lobby. 20 rooms.

Hotel Krafft $$ *Rheingasse 12, tel: 061 690 9130*, www.hotelkrafft.ch. In a building dating from 1872 overlooking the Rhine, all rooms were renovated in 2008. Many have excellent views of the old town and Münster, some with a terrace. 45 rooms.

BERN

Belle Epoque $$$$ *Gerechtigkeitsgasse 18, tel: 031 311 4336*, www.belle-epoque.ch. Situated in the lower part of the old town on one of Bern's most famous streets and just across the bridge from the Bear Pit. This small, charming hotel offers a quiet retreat in tastefully decorated rooms, most with antiques and furnishings from the Belle Epoque. 17 rooms.

Bellevue Palace $$$$$ *Kochergasse 3–5, tel: 031 320 4545*, www.bellevue-palace.ch. Having hosted many dignitaries past and present from around the world, the Bellevue Palace is one of Bern's and Switzerland's top hotels. Old-world charm combines with modern conveniences: many guest rooms have commanding views of the Alps. Excellent terrace restaurant with Alpine views. 130 rooms.

Hotel Bern $$$ *Zeughausgasse 9, tel: 031 329 2222*, www.hotelbern.ch. A conveniently located hotel, just a short walk from the railway station. Caters to a business clientele. 100 rooms.

Hotel Jardin $–$$ *Militärstrasse 38, tel: 031 333 0117*, www.hotel-jardin.ch. In a quiet neighbourhood, just outside of the town centre. Inexpensive option with decent rooms. 18 rooms.

BIEL

Hotel Elite $$$ *Bahnhofstrasse 14, tel: 032 328 7777*, www.hotelelite.ch. An art deco hotel in a 1930s building with recently renovated rooms. Not far from the station. 74 rooms.

CRANS-MONTANA

Hostellerie du Pas de l'Ours $$$$$ *tel: 027 485 9333*, www.pasdelours.ch. Nestling in the popular ski region of Crans-Montana, this Relais and Chateaux chalet offers nine suites with mountain ambience. Indoor and outdoor pools with other wellness options. Closed several months in the late spring and autumn.

DAVOS

Hotel Europe $$$ *Promenade 63, tel: 081 415 4141*, www.europe-davos.ch. Well-equipped and located hotel near ski lifts. Rooms are average but adequate for the price. It has an indoor pool, sauna, several bars and restaurants. 64 rooms.

GENEVA

Des Bergues $$$$$ *quai des Bergues 33, tel: 022 908 7000*, www.fourseasons.com/geneva. One of Geneva's oldest hotels, established on the right bank of the lake in 1834, this hotel was recently purchased and renovated by the Four Seasons group. It continues to be one of the great hotels in Geneva. The public rooms are splendid, and guest rooms are large and tastefully decorated. 103 rooms.

Domaine de Châteauvieux $$$ *Chemin de Châteauvieux 16, Satigny, tel: 022 753 1511*, www.chateauvieux.ch. Positioned among the rolling vineyards just outside Geneva, this charming villa offers a quiet place to relax and enjoy the Swiss countryside and the Geneva wine country. Just a short drive to the heart of the city. 14 rooms.

Hôtel Central $ *rue de la Rôtisserie 2, tel: 022 818 8100*, www.hotel central.ch. A hard-to-find, great-value hotel at the base of old town Geneva. Very basic rooms, but for the price, the location cannot be beaten. Rooms can be a bit small, but even the larger rooms are still very affordable. Reception is on the sixth floor. 40 rooms.

Hôtel Longemalle $$$ *place Longemalle 13, tel: 022 818 6262*, www. longemalle.ch. On the left bank and in the centre of it all, Longemalle provides a nice alternative to its higher-priced competitors. Offering a great location (a short walk to old town and the lake), good service, and well-appointed rooms. 58 rooms.

Hôtel Tiffany $$$$ *20 rue de l'Arquebuse, tel: 022 708 1616*, www. hotel-tiffany.ch. A little off the beaten path, but still just a short walk to the heart of Geneva, this boutique hotel lies in a 19th-century building. The Parisian bistro keeps in tune with the ambiance of the hotel and offers excellent fare. 46 rooms.

GSTAAD

Grand Hotel Bellevue $$$$$ *Untergstaadstrasse 17, tel: 033 748 0000*, www.bellevue-gstaad.ch. Reopened in 2013 after a long renovation, this is one of Gstaad's finest and most popular hotels. Offers top-notch service and an extensive wellness centre with much to offer for relaxation. It also has several good dining options. 57 rooms.

INTERLAKEN

Hotel Interlaken $$$–$$$$ *Höheweg 74, tel: 033 826 6868*, www. interlakenhotel.ch. A historic hotel, the oldest in town, which counts Lord Byron as a previous guest. The inside has been renovated and lacks charm, but rooms are adequate and modern. 60 rooms.

Hotel Lötschberg $–$$ *General Guisan Strasse 31, tel: 033 822 2545*, www.lotschberg.ch. Basic, comfortable rooms. An excellent-value, family-run hotel with a very attentive and helpful staff. They can help you plan many outdoor activities. 19 rooms.

Hotel Victoria-Jungfrau $$$$–$$$$$ *Höheweg 41, tel: 033 828 2828*, www.victoria-jungfrau.ch. The grand dame of Interlaken hotels with a clear view over the park towards to the Eiger and Jungfrau on one side and the Harder mountain on the other. The hotel has three restaurants, one with 16 GaultMillau points, and outstanding spa facilities. There is a wide variety of rooms, traditional and modern, and excellent facilities for children, including a children's hour in the dramatically designed indoor pool. 212 rooms.

LAUSANNE

Beau-Rivage Palace $$$$$ *place du Port 17–19, tel: 021 613 3333*, www.brp.ch. Often voted one of the finest hotels in Europe, this 'palace' has been host to famous personalites from around the world since the mid-19th century. Located in Ouchy, on the lakefront. 169 rooms.

Hôtel Angleterre and Résidence $$$$ *Place du Port 11, tel: 021 613 3434*, www.angleterre-residence.ch. Perfectly situated near the shores of Lake Geneva, this modern hotel consists of six buildings, both old and new. Right next to and owned by the Beau-Rivage, guests can use the fitness facilities at its bigger and more expensive neighbour for a small fee. 75 rooms.

Hotel Regina $$$ *rue Grand Saint-Jean 18, tel: 021 320 2441*, www.hotel-regina.ch. This hotel is located in the old town, in a largely pedestrian area. Affordable rooms and very friendly and helpful staff. 36 rooms.

LEUKERBAD

Heliopark Hotels and Alpentherme $$$ *Dorfplatz 1, tel: 027 472 1000*, www.heliopark.ch. Large resort hotel with indoor and outdoor thermal baths and a variety of other wellness options. 135 rooms.

Hotel Belvedere $$$ *Via ai Monti della Trinità 44, tel: 091 751 0363*, www.belvedere-locarno.ch. Renovated mansion located on a hill overlooking Locarno and Lake Maggiore. All guest rooms offer views of the lake and most of them come with balconies. 80 rooms.

Hotel Dell'Angelo $ *Piazza Grande, tel: 091 751 8175*, www.hotel-dell-angelo.ch. Inexpensive, family-run hotel in the centre of Locarno. Friendly, helpful staff. 55 rooms.

Hotel Krone $$$ *Weinmarkt 12, tel: 041 419 4400*, http://krone-luzern.ch. A simple, no-frills option overlooking the Weinmarkt square in the old town. Rooms are clean and modern. Good value, especially for the location. 25 rooms.

The Hotel $$$$ *Sempacherstrasse 14, tel: 041 226 8686*, www.the-hotel.ch. One of Switzerland's most distinctive hotels, this so-called 'deluxe boutique' hotel mixes modern conveniences with a chic atmosphere. Designed by Jean Nouvel, who designed Lucerne's new convention centre. 30 rooms.

Wilden Mann $$$–$$$$ *Bahnhofstrasse 30, tel: 041 210 1666*, www.wilden-mann.ch. With traditional décor and old-world charm, the Wilden Mann combines seven old townhouses to create one of Lucerne's most famous hotels. The name comes from the 'Wild Man' symbol of medieval folklore and the hotel creates a rustic ambiance befitting an ancient myth. 50 rooms.

Hotel International au Lac $$–$$$ *Via Nassa 68, tel: 091 922 7541*, www.hotel-international.ch. Operated by the same family since 1906, this reasonably priced hotel is ideally situated in the centre of Lugano and by the lake. Only open Easter–October. 80 rooms.

Principe Leopoldo and Residence $$$$ *Via Montalbano 5, tel: 091 985 8855*, www.leopoldohotel.com. Built by Prussian Prince Frederic Leopold, this is one of Lugano's top and most interesting hotels. The rooms and suites are combined into two buildings on Lugano's 'Golden Hill'. Extensive fitness options including two pools and spa. 78 rooms.

Romantik Hotel Ticino $$$$ *Piazza Cioccaro 1, tel: 091 922 7772*, www.ticinohotel.ch. Close to the lake in the centre of Lugano, this small hotel offers comfortable rooms in a relaxed setting, with a peaceful courtyard. Closed January and first part of February. 18 rooms.

MONTREUX

Eden Palace au Lac $$$–$$$$ *rue du Théâtre 11, tel: 021 966 0800*, www.edenpalace.ch. Not as luxurious or as expensive as some of its neighbours along the lake in Montreux, but a nonetheless elegant hotel offering great views of Lake Geneva and the Alps. 110 rooms.

MÜRREN

Hotel Edelwiess $ *Hauptstrasse, tel: 033 856 5600*, www.edelweiss-muerren.ch. Superbly situated hotel in this car-free resort with stupendous views over the Lauterbrunnen valley towards the Jungfrau and Eiger. It has attractive, traditionally furnished rooms and a restaurant which offers much of the same decor. 24 rooms.

MURTEN

Hotel Adler $ *Hauptgasse 45, tel: 026 672 6669*, www.adler-hotel. ch. Quaint, old, family-run hotel that has a selection of charming, imaginatively decorated rooms named after the famous guests who have stayed here, Goethe and Casanova among them. Unbeatable location in the heart of the old town, a few minutes' stroll from the lake. 24 rooms.

NEUCHÂTEL

La Maison du Prussien $$ *rue des Tunnels 11, tel: 032 730 5454,* www.hotel-prussien.ch. In an old brewery from the 18th century, this quaint hotel is tucked away among the trees in a natural setting that contains a stream and old mills. A little hard to find, but decent value in an interesting location. 10 rooms.

PONTRESINA

Hotel Müller $$$ *Via Maistra 202, tel: 081 839 3000,* www.hotel-mueller.ch. Century-old hotel renovated in 2005. Small with bright, modern rooms. Italian restaurant. 18 rooms.

ST-GALLEN

Einstein $$$–$$$$ *Berneggstrasse 2, tel: 071 227 5555,* www.einstein.ch. Named after a textile manufacturer, the Einstein served as an embroidery factory and a charity among other things before being transformed into a hotel in the early 1980s. Modern, comfortable rooms near the abbey. 113 rooms.

ST MORITZ

Hotel Soldanella $$$–$$$$ *Via Somplaz 17, tel: 081 830 8500,* www.hotel-soldanella.ch. A nice, affordable option for St Moritz, which has many upscale choices. The Soldanella provides clean, modern rooms and a wellness centre for relaxation. Some rooms come with fantastic views of the Engadine mountains. 36 rooms. Closed several months during late spring and autumn.

Suvretta House $$$$–$$$$$ *Via Chasellas 1, tel: 081 836 3636,* www.suvrettahouse.ch. One of St Moritz's grand hotels, the Suvretta's location is undeniably special. The hotel has a park-like setting and their own ski-lift is nearby, so outdoor activities are easily accessible. They even have their own ski school, curling surface and skating rink. 189 rooms. Closed several months during late spring and autumn.

SCHAFFHAUSEN

Sorell Hotel Rüden $$$ *Oberstadt 20 tel: 052 632 3636,* https://sorell hotels.com. Located in a former guildhouse, the hotel has a deceivingly modern interior. Centrally located, there are many dining options within walking distance. Very hospitable staff. Ask for a room not facing the station.

SOLOTHURN

Zunfthaus zu Wirthen $$ *Hauptgasse 41, tel: 032 626 28 48,* www.wirthen.ch. This small, family-run hotel is located in the centre of the town. Friendly staff and great food in the restaurant downstairs. 16 rooms.

WENGEN

Hotel Caprice $$$$ *Postfach 244, tel: 033 856 0606,* www.caprice-wengen.ch. A new building (1989) that blends effortlessly into the Alpine scenery outside and features modern rooms and conveniences. Located near the town centre and close to the slopes. Closed for several months during Spring and Autumn. 18 rooms.

ZERMATT

Coeur des Alpes $$$–$$$$ *Oberdorfstrasse 134, tel: 027 966 4080,* www.coeurdesalpes.ch. A combination of Swiss chalet (exposed wood beams) and modern décor (with a glass-floor lounge that looks down into the spa). Small, with seven suites and six double rooms. Consider the Penthouse Suite, which has magnificent views of the Matterhorn.

Hotel Daniela $$ *Steinmattstrasse 39, tel: 027 966 7700,* www.hotel daniela.ch. An inexpensive option that is great value compared to the usually higher-priced Zermatt hotels and inns. Guests are welcome to use the wellness centre at its sister hotel, the Julen (www.julen.ch), which is a little more expensive and just a short walk away. 24 rooms.

The Omnia $$$$$ *Auf dem Fels, tel: 027 966 7171*, www.the-omnia. com. A mountain-lodge-style hotel with all modern conveniences, situated just above Zermatt. Pool, outdoor Jacuzzi, and other wellness options.

ZURICH

Greulich Hotel $$ *Herman-Greulich-Strasse 56, tel: 043 243 4243*, www.greulich.ch. A small hotel in a quiet neighbourhood with a peaceful inner courtyard and modern design. Just outside the city centre. 18 rooms.

Hotel Adler $$ *Rosengasse 10, tel: 044 266 9696*, www.hotel-adler. ch. Renovated hotel with basic, modern rooms. Located on the right bank, in the heart of the old town. Great value and location for exploring Zurich. Popular restaurant, Swiss Chuchi, serves traditional Swiss fare. 52 rooms.

Hotel Hirschen $$ *Niederdorfstrasse 13, tel: 043 268 3333*, www. hirschen-zuerich.ch. Affordable hotel with modern, comfortable rooms just steps away from the Limmat river on the right bank. The walls of the famous wine cellar, Weinschenke, date back to the 16th century. 27 rooms.

Hotel Florhof $$$$ *Florhofgasse 4, tel: 044 250 2626*, www.hotel florhof.ch. Situated on a quiet street on the right bank of the lake, this former merchant's house has been transformed into a quaint boutique hotel with an excellent restaurant. Consider the junior suites if you desire a little more space. 33 rooms.

Widder Hotel $$$$$ *Rennweg 7, tel: 044 224 2526*, www.widderhotel. ch. One of Zurich's finest and most famous hotels, the Widder comprises no less than eight interconnected historic townhouses in the heart of Zurich. Each building was remodelled in a unique fashion and the rooms are decorated individually as well, so that no two are alike. Seven suites available, some with a rooftop terrace. 49 rooms.

INDEX